SHARPENING THE DEVELOPMENT PROCESS

Introducing the Praxis Series

INTRAC launched the Praxis programme in 2003, with an overall aim to help strengthen the capacity of civil society organisations (CSOs), non-governmental organisations (NGOs), and other agencies who support them. Praxis expects to highlight new, interesting and alternative practice in the provision of capacity building support, through an integration of research, consultation, participation and reflection with practitioners, academics and decision makers in a continuous action learning spiral.

The programme will focus on three inter-related themes: Developing Process and Practice; Transferability and Applicability; and Impact Assessment. These will be addressed through diverse activities including a global Action Learning Network, several international workshops and conferences, support for exchanges and fellowships, a research fund for partners, commissioned research, and a new Praxis Series. The Praxis Series will include a range of practical guides, of which this is the first, together with thought pieces, commentaries and research reports. These will be complemented by publications on the web, such as articles and other work in progress, including items in translation.

The Praxis team will be developing a contact list for those interested in the themes and activities outlined above, as a vehicle for the dissemination of ideas, events, publications and other news. If you wish to be added to the listings, or consult current details of the programme, please view the INTRAC website at www.intrac.org or email: info.praxis@intrac.org.

SHARPENING THE

A Practical Guide to Monitoring and Evaluation

DEVELOPMENT PROCESS

Oliver Bakewell

with Jerry Adams & Brian Pratt

 Publication

INTRAC:

The International Non-governmental Organisation Training and Research Centre

A Summary Description

INTRAC was set up in 1991 to provide specially designed management, training and research services for NGOs involved in relief and development in the South and dedicated to improving organisational effectiveness and programme performance of Northern NGOs and Southern partners where appropriate. Our goal is to serve NGOs in (i) the exploration of the management, policy and human resource issues affecting their own organisational development, and (ii) the evolution of more effective programmes of institutional development and co-operation.

INTRAC offers the complementary services of:
Training;
Consultancy; and
Research.

First published in 2003 in the UK by
INTRAC
PO Box 563
Oxford
OX2 6RZ
United Kingdom

Tel: +44 (0)1865 201851
Fax: +44 (0)1865 201852
e-mail: info@intrac.org
website: www.intrac.org

ISBN 1-897748-78-7

Designed and produced by
Jerry Burman
Tel: 01803 409754

Printed in Great Britain by
Antony Rowe Ltd., Chippenham, Wiltshire

Contents

Acknowledgements

As noted in the Foreword, this book does draw freely on material which INTRAC has in-house. Much of this has been largely rewritten but there is a large debt to the authors who have gone before. In particular, the work of Brian Pratt, Jerry Adams and the late Peter Oakley should be acknowledged. Other work is acknowledged by references in the main text.

Foreword

This book has been written to help those who are committed to social development to assess the progress of development programmes. Perhaps you are working for an organisation which is running various social development initiatives in a particular area or country. You will want to know what your work is achieving and if you could do things better. If you are living in a community where social development programmes are being implemented possibly by government departments, non-governmental organisations or a community based organisation, you may want to know what these programmes are offering and what difference they are making. If you are providing funds to another organisation to undertake development activities in an area, you will want to know if your money is being well used and what it is achieving.

Continuous monitoring of the work and periodic evaluations can help to answer such questions. This guide introduces the basic ideas of monitoring and evaluation and gives simple guidelines for setting up a system for monitoring and evaluation. It has been written particularly with field workers in mind, either in small organisations with a limited number of projects or programmes, or the field managers of large organisations. These may include both those who are new to the systematic use of monitoring and evaluation in their work, and those who are trying to get to grips with the existing practice of monitoring and evaluation within their organisation. At times this book may help reinforce such practices and at others it may challenge them.

We recognise that there is a wide variety of organisations involved in social development including small community based organisations, large and small national and international non-governmental organisations (NGOs), UN bodies, donors and private companies. In anticipation that the majority of the readers of this guide will be involved in NGOs, where there are references to a specific type of organisation in the text, the example used is generally that of a Southern NGO. The aim of this is to make the text consistent and there is no intention to exclude those from other backgrounds.

We face a similar difficulty in establishing the object of monitoring and evaluation for the purpose of this book. It is still the case that the basic unit for the majority of social development interventions is the project. Projects may be gathered together in programmes or sectors. We may be concerned about the implications of adopting a particular strategy or management structure. We may be interested in the processes of change which underlie our rationale for intervention. The principles of monitoring and evaluation described in this book can be applied in these different areas. Since projects remain the basic unit and they are the simplest to deal with in this introductory guide, we focus on projects for the examples in this book.

INTRAC has gained considerable experience of monitoring and evaluation over many years. It has arranged a series of five evaluation conferences over the past ten years which have brought together practitioners and academics from the around world to discuss developments in the theory and practice of evaluation. It has also built up a large collection of material and case studies through its research and consultancy with a wide range of organisations, including NGOs, donors and UN bodies. Some of this material has been published as books and working papers.

Although these and many other published resources make a valuable contribution to the body of knowledge on monitoring and evaluation, they are not sufficiently geared towards helping people starting in the practice. This book draws heavily on INTRAC's previous work but aims more explicitly to give practical guidelines. In particular, it tries to unpack some of the ideas which are used freely when talking of monitoring and evaluation but rarely explained in practical terms for the novice. For example, what is a *terms of reference*? what do we actually mean when we talk about *data analysis* and how do we do it?

This is an *introductory* guide and does not claim to be last word on monitoring and evaluation. In order to make the book accessible to a wide audience both in language and price, we have aimed to keep the text short and concise. At times this means that only limited details are given or alternative ways of doing things are not covered in any detail. We have attempted to provide appropriate references in the text and bibliography to help the reader who wishes to find out more. We have included some internet resources, which may be more readily available where book shops or libraries are not common.

The Organisation of this Guide

This guide is divided into three parts:

* Guidelines for Monitoring and Evaluation – this provides the basic framework for establishing a monitoring and evaluation system;

* Managing Information – this gives more details about common ways of managing information for monitoring and evaluation

* Monitoring and Evaluation for Advocacy, Capacity Building and Humanitarian Emergencies.

The first part starts by discussing the different approaches to monitoring and evaluation and introduces some basic principles for the 'interpretive' approach which is adopted in this guide – drawing on a wide range of views of a programme rather than relying on data provided by experts. It then lays some groundwork for establishing a monitoring and evaluation system by looking at its relationship with planning, and introducing indicators and baselines.

Some guidelines for setting up a monitoring system for social development projects are then offered. These raise particular issues which must be considered such as: the information to be used; the people to be involved in monitoring; and, the system for managing monitoring information. The following chapter looks at evaluation including the purposes of and criteria for evaluation and providing practical guidelines for setting up and managing an evaluation.

The second part of the book focuses on managing information in monitoring and evaluation systems. Information is a vital ingredient of both monitoring and evaluation. Although there are some differences in the type of data and techniques used for both processes, there is no sharp line to draw between them. Rather than try to ascribe particular methods to either monitoring or evaluation, instead we save the details of managing information to the second part of the book. This looks in turn at different types of data, how to choose what data is required, and ways of collecting and analysing it to ensure that it is useful.

These first two sections provide the core of the book, which we hope will cover many different areas of social development. In addition, in Part 3, we discuss three areas of work which do not so easily fit into the framework: advocacy, capacity building and humanitarian emergencies. The difficulties of monitoring and evaluation in these three fields are highlighted there.

PART 1

Guidelines for Monitoring and Evaluation

In this first part of the guide, we focus on the design of a monitoring and evaluation system for organisations engaged in social development projects. Chapter 1 gives a broad overview of the system, discusses some of the theoretical issues and makes the link between monitoring and evaluation systems and project planning. Chapters 2 and 3 focus on more practical guidelines for establishing a monitoring system and running evaluations, respectively. The details of dealing with data are left to the second part of the book.

Chapter 1 introduces the concepts of monitoring and evaluation and clarifies the distinction between the two. Some of the different approaches to monitoring and evaluation are then presented. This book takes a pluralist approach, which respects the views of different stakeholders and looks at both monitoring and evaluation as processes of negotiation to a consensus view. This provides the basis for some principles underlying the monitoring and evaluation system. The rest of the chapter is concerned with relating the monitoring and evaluation system to the overall project cycle and the aims and objectives of the project. This involves briefly introducing the idea of indicators and the baseline which is established as a project starts.

Chapter 2 expands on the definition of monitoring and provides some guidelines for establishing a monitoring system, including what information is required, who should be involved and how information will be used. Managing data is a major challenge for any monitoring system and some practical guidelines for recording and storing information are provided.

Chapter 3 focuses on evaluation and describes the different types and purposes of evaluation. It then provides practical guidelines on how to set up an evaluation, including drawing up the terms of reference, putting together an evaluation team and managing an evaluation from first preparation to reviewing the process.

CHAPTER 1

Monitoring and Evaluation Systems

An organisation which is carrying out any activity needs to have some system in place to ensure that its work is going according to plan, and to identify and solve problems as they occur. The most basic example is that of financial monitoring. This is required to check that the organisation has sufficient funds at any time to purchase inputs, pay suppliers and staff, and to check that all money is accounted for and none is misused. Such a financial monitoring system is required by every organisation, whether a business or development agency.

In addition, an organisation will want to take stock of its position from time to time. In the case of a business, it may want to see how far it has grown, if it is meeting its customers' needs and what lessons have been learnt from experience. Again, the most common form of review is that given in the annual accounts. Investors, staff and customers will look at such accounts as they make decisions about their future involvement in the company.

Development organisations should have such financial systems in place as a matter of course, but they are concerned about much more than just their finances. People engage in development activities in order to bring about positive changes to address particular problems. These may be problems they face themselves, in the case of community organisations, or problems faced by others in the case of external development agencies. A strong monitoring and evaluation system will help to ensure that
the work is going in the right direction.

Source: Feuerstein 1986:19

In this chapter the basic groundwork for monitoring and evaluation systems is laid out. We look at the purpose and definitions of monitoring and evaluation and outline some of the different approaches to them. The relationship between project planning and monitoring and evaluation is explored and some of the basic concepts used are introduced.

Why Monitor and Evaluate?

It is important for all concerned in social development projects that their work is continuously monitored and regularly evaluated for the following reasons:

Accountability

This is often seen as the most important reason for monitoring and evaluating development programmes. In every case, those who are implementing the programmes are carrying out work on behalf of others and it is important to be confident that they are working responsibly, i.e. they are accountable.

Accountability works in two directions:

Accountability to donors – many social development programmes are supported by funds from donors who want to know how the money is used. Increasingly they also want to know whether the work they support is having the desired effect. Many Northern NGO donors are under increasing pressure from their own donors, especially where these are governments, to increase and improve their level of accountability. Monitoring and evaluation can justify the allocation of scarce resources to the project.

Accountability to project users – those involved in social development are acting on behalf of others, either as representatives of the community which is expected to benefit from the project, or as an external organisation which is aiming to support the development process. In either case, the people running the project have a responsibility to show the people they serve what they have been doing and to explain their actions. Donors are likely to give resources to an organisation to work on the community's behalf; the community is entitled to know what resources have been given and how those resources have been used.

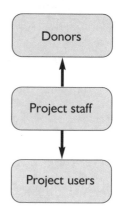

Figure 1: *Lines of accountability*

Examples:

An NGO building a school classroom is accountable for the quality of the building to ensure that it is of appropriate standards and is safe.

An NGO providing training for the unemployed to help them obtain jobs should provide training which is appropriate and gives relevant skills.

There is often less pressure to improve the accountability of NGOs to project users than to donors. This means that an NGO may be less accountable or responsive to these users than the government and the commercial sector – poor service leads to elections being lost by governments or reduced sales and profits for businesses.[1] There may be no similar penalty for an NGO which is doing a bad job. Many NGOs offer services as a monopoly – project users either take the poor quality service they are offered or leave it and do without any service. There is little competition (at the level of the beneficiary as opposed to the income sources) and few ways of dissatisfaction being signalled back to NGO managers. Monitoring and evaluation can help to create this feedback loop, hence the growing interest in participatory methods which capture client views and perceptions.

Improving Performance

This is an equally important reason for setting up a monitoring and evaluation system, although some see it as secondary to ensuring accountability. Ongoing monitoring will show how resources are being used and highlight problems as they occur so that they can be addressed. Issues raised by monitoring may include concerns about day to day management such as inefficient use of staff, or signs that the project is (or is not) producing the outputs that it planned and that they are achieving the desired results.

Examples:

Monitoring how many people took part in meetings showed that more women came when meetings were held on Sunday afternoons rather than weekday evenings. Moving more meetings to Sundays helped the organisation improve the participation of women in the project.

Routine monitoring of people's attitudes to community health workshops run by an NGO showed that many were not putting the lessons into practice in their homes. This prompted the NGO to review the content and delivery of its health education material.

Periodic evaluations can improve performance by taking an overall view of a project's achievements and direction (drawing in monitoring data) and making recommendations for changes in the light of experience.

Learning

As well as improving performance in an individual project, monitoring and evaluation can also provide valuable lessons for other projects within the same organisation or those run

---

[1] See Fowler (1997).

by other organisations in the same sector or location. These lessons may be applied to existing projects or to those which start in the future to help them repeat successes or avoid failures.

Not only do the results of monitoring and evaluation contribute to learning, but also the process of carrying out monitoring and evaluation can help staff and project participants develop new skills:

- Stakeholders' involvement in monitoring and evaluation can increase their motivation to participate in planning and implementing future activities.

- By assessing achievements and problems, participants in monitoring and evaluation enhance their analytical capacity and critical awareness.

Communication

Monitoring and evaluation can help increase the communication between different stakeholders by exposing them to each other's perspectives on an intervention. This may be closely related to learning but it may also extend to those who have no direct influence on the implementation of the project. Thus clients may learn something about the donor agency, the Northern public may learn more about the reality of the people they are supporting, either through donations to an NGO or their taxes. To succeed in this, the monitoring and evaluation should be carried out in such a way that the different stakeholders do not feel threatened, so they can openly discuss successes and problems faced by the project.

Definitions of Monitoring and Evaluation

So far we have mostly talked about monitoring and evaluation as if they are virtually the same. Before proceeding further, it is important to make clear the difference between the two terms. In this book we take the definitions of monitoring and evaluation to be as follows:

Monitoring is the systematic and continuous assessment of the progress of a piece of work over time, which checks that things are 'going to plan' and enables adjustments to be made in a methodical way.[2]

It has often been said that monitoring is concerned with looking at the project's activities and outputs rather than its overall objectives and the changes brought about by the project.[3] In this book we reject this view and argue that it is just as important continuously to

---

[2] Drawn from Gosling and Edwards (1995: 81); Blankenberg 1995: 413.
[3] E.g. Cracknell (2000: 165).

monitor what the project is achieving as it is to monitor what it is doing.

Monitoring is an integral part of the management system and will generally be carried out by those involved in the project from day to day. At the least this will involve the project staff, but it is even better if the project users also participate in monitoring.

The process of monitoring will include a wide range of meetings, workshops and other activities, which should contribute to accountability, improved performance, learning and communication. The tangible outputs, which should capture much of this process, will include regular reports such as monthly field reports, quarterly reports to the organisation's senior management and annual reports to other stakeholders such as project users, relevant government departments and donors.

Evaluation is the periodic assessment of the relevance, performance, efficiency and impact of a piece of work with respect to its stated objectives.[4] An evaluation is usually carried out at some significant stage in the project's development, e.g. at the end of a planning period, as the project moves to a new phase, or in response to a particular critical issue.

An evaluation will measure what progress the project has made, not only in completing its activities but also in achieving its objectives and overall goal. It will assess what changes have occurred as a result of the project taking place – both those changes which were planned and also those which were unexpected.

An evaluation will usually involve people who are not directly engaged in the day to day running of the project as well as a wide range of stakeholders. Often the evaluation may be led by a person who is external to the organisation such as specialist consultant, but at times it may be appropriate for an organisation to arrange an internal evaluation using its own staff. Whoever is leading the evaluation, it should be participatory and involve all stakeholders – especially project users and staff – at all stages from design to conclusion.

Like monitoring, the process of evaluation is likely to be an end in itself and will result in improved accountability, performance, learning and communication. The output of an evaluation may include a one off report prepared by the evaluation team, which will describe the evaluation's findings and present recommendations for immediate and future changes within the project and the organisations involved. In the process of preparing this report, the evaluation team should hold a number of workshops or other meetings with stakeholders to present draft findings in order to ensure that the final report takes into account their views.

These differences between monitoring and evaluation are summarised in Table 1. In this book we differentiate between monitoring and evaluation only according to how they are carried out and at what point in the project cycle. However, we assume that both practices are concerned with answering questions about outputs, objectives and impacts. Experience has shown that it is very difficult to assess progress in achieving objectives in

---

[4] Drawn from Casley and Kumar (1987), Gosling and Edwards (1995: 89).

Table 1: *Summary of differences between monitoring and evaluation*

	Monitoring	Evaluation
Timing	Continuous throughout the project	Periodic review at significant point in project progress – end of project, mid point of project, change of phase
Scope	Day to day activities, outputs, indicators of progress and change	Assess overall delivery of outputs and progress towards objectives and goal
Main participants	Project staff, project users	External evaluators/ facilitators, project users, project staff, donors
Process	Regular meetings, interviews – monthly, quarterly reviews etc.	Extraordinary meetings, additional data collection exercises etc.
Written outputs	Regular reports and updates to project users, management and donors	Written report with recommendations for changes to project – presented in workshops to different stakeholders

periodic evaluations if information has not been collected throughout the project's operation. It is even harder to understand the project's impact unless changes have been regularly monitored.[5]

Different Approaches to Monitoring and Evaluation

As part of the groundwork for designing a monitoring and evaluation system it is essential to understand something of the theoretical basis on which the project rests. Behind every social development project is a conceptual framework – a way of viewing the world and making sense of it which brings with it a particular understanding of the way people behave and social changes occur. This conceptual framework will make a difference to the way that social problems are analysed and the resultant projects designed to address them (see Box 1).

Over time, as new conceptual frameworks have evolved, there have been many changes in the approaches towards social development. These have been reflected in way that monitoring and evaluation is carried out. There is still considerable debate about good practice in monitoring and evaluation and there is no one 'best practice'. There is a range of views of how the development process should be monitored and evaluated and the two extremes can be described as technocratic and pluralist:

---

[5] Note that similar distinctions between monitoring and evaluation can be drawn where the object is a programme, sector or strategy, rather than a project. For example, if we are looking at the implementation of a strategy, the scope of monitoring may be concerned with incremental changes within the organisation (new management systems etc.), while an evaluation may look at how these organisational changes work out to affect the lives of those involved in the development work of the organisation.

Box 1: *Making the conceptual framework clear*

'Underlying social development is always an implicit or explicit understanding that development is about social change or transformation. It is argued here that it is not possible to evaluate social development without being clear of the conceptual basis upon which the social development programme is built. An essential part of the pre-planning for the evaluation will be to identify as far as possible the conceptual, theoretical and even ideological foundations or origins from which the programme has emerged'. (Marsden et al. 1994: 119).

For example, one person may take the view of the world being an arena of competing interests where it must be assumed that, as a general rule, different groups do things in ways to maximise their own interests. Therefore, the world can be seen as inevitably in conflict and the role of social development is to help the weak overcome the oppression of the strong.

Another person may understand the world as one where people's position is determined by chance and what is holding them back is their lack of access to education and new technology.

Two people with these different views may interpret the same facts about food shortage differently. The former may come up with a project focused on improving people's rights and access to resources (land, water, agricultural inputs). The latter may design a project more concerned with technical advice to improve farmer's skills in dealing with water conservation, soil erosion, storage.

Different organisations will operate with different conceptual frameworks and there may be various conceptual frameworks in different projects within the same organisation. If the basic model of social change underlying the project can be made clear, it will help all the stakeholders understand better what the project is trying to achieve and why. This will make monitoring and evaluation easier.

- *Technocratic* – based on the view that, with the right resources, science and technology will provide the solutions to all human problems and their progress can be monitored and evaluated using mechanisms that are objective and value neutral. For example, in this approach evaluations *should* be carried out by an external evaluator who will judge the project's progress in a scientific way against set criteria.

  This view tends to assume that the techniques for achieving successful development are known and shortfalls in the projects are likely to lie in poor management. The results of monitoring and evaluation are likely to be fine tuning rather than any major revision of the project's assumptions, perceptions or design. The technocratic approach will often involve an increase in managerial control and a drive towards standardisation through the preparation of manuals and operating procedures so that successful projects can be replicated.

- *Pluralist* – this approach is based on a pluralistic view of development which holds that different perceptions of reality should be treated with respect and considered in their own right rather than having one scientific correct answer. It believes that different stakeholders will have different perspectives on the world in general and development projects in particular. Thus success or failure will mean different things to different observers. A successful agricultural project as defined by an agronomist, which increases yields through the use of a hybrid, may be a disaster to local women who find the hybrid is less useful for brewing, which provides an important supplement to their income.

This means that there are no absolute or objective criteria for monitoring and evaluation which can be set by planners or evaluators in advance from outside. It also means that due to the perceptions of evaluators having their own social and cultural origins evaluations are never neutral. An evaluator therefore should aim to provide an interpretation of events rather than a judgement. The evaluation process is therefore designed to provide space for dialogue between stakeholders rather than produce a report which gives merely the views of the evaluators.

Clearly these two approaches are set out as extreme ends of a spectrum and there is plenty of middle ground between them. As views have moved along this spectrum, there has been a noticeable shift over time in the style of monitoring and evaluation used within public life, which has been described as passing through four generations[6]:

- *Measurement* – first generation: dominated by quantitative measurement and emphasis on facts with a stress on individual people or objects. E.g. for water supply, how many wells, how much water; for literacy, how many words can someone read.

- *Description* – second generation: more descriptive and looking at the progress of the whole project against its objectives. E.g. for water supply, assess the number and quality of wells covering an area; for literacy, review general progress in the classes, type of curriculum.

- *Judgement* – third generation: assesses the effects of development interventions and looks to establish whether an approach succeeded or failed and reasons for it. Tends to look beyond individual projects to programmes. E.g. for water supply, assess overall changes in district water supply to see if development interventions are causing improvement; for literacy, assess changes in levels of literacy in areas.

- *Interpretive* – fourth generation: involves range of stakeholders in assessing their different views of the project's progress and impact and negotiating a consensus for its future development. E.g. for water supply, listen to view of women who may no longer have to walk long distances for water, children who may have to wait for a long time by the new tap, to health workers who record changes in water borne diseases etc.; for literacy, listen to views of progress from teachers, learners, employers etc. and look at how the new skill is used.

---

[6] See Guba and Lincoln (1989).

The first three generations rely more heavily on the views of project management and evaluators at the expense of other stakeholders, who tend to be disempowered. The approach taken in this book is primarily 'interpretive' to the extent that we stress the need to obtain a wide range of opinions and perceptions about a programme and not to depend purely on data collected by experts such as staff or other internal recording/monitoring systems.

Basic Principles for a Monitoring and Evaluation System

In order to develop a monitoring and evaluation system for social development activities that is consistent with an interpretive approach, the experiences of many NGOs and other development organisations suggest that the following basic principles should apply:

- *Participatory* – the system should be based upon the participation of as wide a range of stakeholders as is realistically possible and the contributions of the various groups should be valued (see Box 2);

- *Minimum but cost effective* – it should not be over-complicated and should be understandable to both staff and project partners at all levels and should not require time consuming or unnecessary reporting;

- *Producing consistent, good quality information* – on output, outcome and impact to feed into the project cycle – both for accountability and learning purposes – leading to the ongoing adaptation of plans and objectives;

- *Gender aware* – women's as well as men's concerns and experiences must be an integral part of the monitoring and evaluation system. Data must be disaggregated by gender and the different impact of projects on women and men must be considered. The gender implications of changes to the project arising from monitoring and evaluation must be assessed to ensure that both women and men benefit equally and inequality is not perpetuated.

- *Building capacity* – the system should be designed in such a way that it uses and develops the capacity of those involved for reflection on the project's progress and analysis of the monitoring and evaluation data;

- *Emphasising analysis and decision making* – the system should not merely be focused on the collection of data but ensure that information is analysed and used in decision making;

- *Including unintended consequences* – the system should not assume that the outcomes and impact resulting from the project are limited to those anticipated in the project but it should be able to record and analyse changes which were not expected;

- *Open to alternative sources of information* – the system should acknowledge the value of different types of information, both oral and visual, and of the perceptions of local people who have not been directly involved in the project.

Recent research and experience in social development practice[7] has shown that it is necessary to adopt a *process* approach to monitoring and evaluation in order to follow these principles. A process approach does not rigidly define all the key elements in the monitoring and evaluation system at the start of a project or programme; instead the system evolves out of the ongoing experience of implementing the project. In this approach stakeholders, and particularly the primary ones, have a key role since they are not used simply as the objects of exercises seeking to verify quantitative change, but more importantly they themselves suggest and describe the changes which may have taken place. Furthermore, a process approach will also continually examine the assumptions on which the project was based and change tack accordingly, and not merely crunch out the numbers. In a process approach the use of informal (often oral) information is important, since it is quicker and can often influence day to day decisions.

For a monitoring and evaluation system to evaluate qualitative change and the impact of interventions, it is essential that it is built around the participation of stakeholders at all levels. People's perceptions and experiences must lie at the heart of such a system. Local people must routinely be involved in identifying changes which are occurring and in understanding their impact and significance. Understanding sustainable changes in people's lives must take account of their values and priorities; projects cannot be deemed to have positively affected the lives of local people if the perceptions of the local people diverge seriously from those of external observers. In certain circumstances this may mean the deliberate playing down of the kinds of data and information which formal evaluations usually value and putting more emphasis on people's ideas on the changes which have occurred. Monitoring may be a formal process, but local people also continually monitor events and change in their particular way.

Relationship Between Planning, Monitoring and Evaluation

Before any development initiative is started there will be a planning process which should ideally include all stakeholders. A major part of the planning will be to understand what development problem the project is hoping to address and how the project is expected to bring improvements. Any programme or project plan should include some statement of the problems, an analysis, which shows potential solutions, and a description of what the project will be doing to contribute to a solution. It is also very important that the proposal should describe what evidence will be used to demonstrate that the project is actually doing what it set out to do, and that this is achieving the desired results.

---

[7] See Oakley et al. (1998), Mikkelsen (1995: 166ff).

Box 2: *Participation and inclusion*

Participation must be a basic building block of the approach to monitoring and evaluation rather than just rhetoric. It will not be achieved instantly but will increase and deepen as local people gain confidence and become more involved in monitoring and evaluation. Various studies describe the process as having a number of different stages*. One the simplest is the four stage model adopted by the World Bank:

The Process of Participation	
Passive participation ⇩	Where stakeholders simply respond to requests for information and have no other role in monitoring and evaluation.
Increasing involvement ⇩	Where stakeholders volunteer information and express interest in how it is used.
Active participation ⇩	Where stakeholders are involved in deciding what information should be collected, methods used and the analysis of the data.
Ownership/empowerment	Where stakeholders play a key role in selecting the criteria and indicators for measuring project progress and call staff to account for the project's performance.

It is very important that participation is an inclusive process and is not restricted to dominant stakeholders who have the loudest voices. It is essential that the monitoring and evaluation system describes the impact on all key stakeholders' parties to ensure that there is an equitable distribution of benefits and the project does not contribute to inequality which is often at the heart of people's poverty.

The project's potential impact on gender relations should have been considered in the project planning, and it is essential that this is followed through to the monitoring and evaluation. In particular, women must be full participants in the monitoring and evaluation system to ensure that their views are taken on board and the impact of the project on women and men is disaggregated. Women and men are likely to have different areas of knowledge and information systems – for example, women tend to have more knowledge of the specific gender differentiated socio-economic indicators that define vulnerable households.

It is also important to ensure that people from different ethnic groups, socio-economic classes and ages are fully included in the design and operation of the monitoring and evaluation system.

* Biggs 1994, Save the Children 1994, UNDP 2000 *Empowering People A Guide to Participation*, UNDP guidebook

In other words, the way that a project or programme will be monitored and evaluated must be considered at the design and planning stage. In preparing a project framework it is normal to consider what indicators should be used and these often form the first criteria against which the project's progress will be measured. It is also important to consider the following factors:

- If changes are to be observed it will be important to record the situation before the project starts.

- If the project's progress towards its outputs, objectives and goal is to be monitored and evaluated, these must be clearly defined.

- For monitoring to be incorporated within the management of the project, it must be present from the beginning.

- In order to develop a participatory monitoring and evaluation system which includes the beneficiaries, they must be involved in deciding what changes should be monitored.

When monitoring you will check up on the progress of a project while it is continuing and you will want to identify what is going well and what is going badly. If things are going

Figure 2: *Links between planning, monitoring and evaluation*

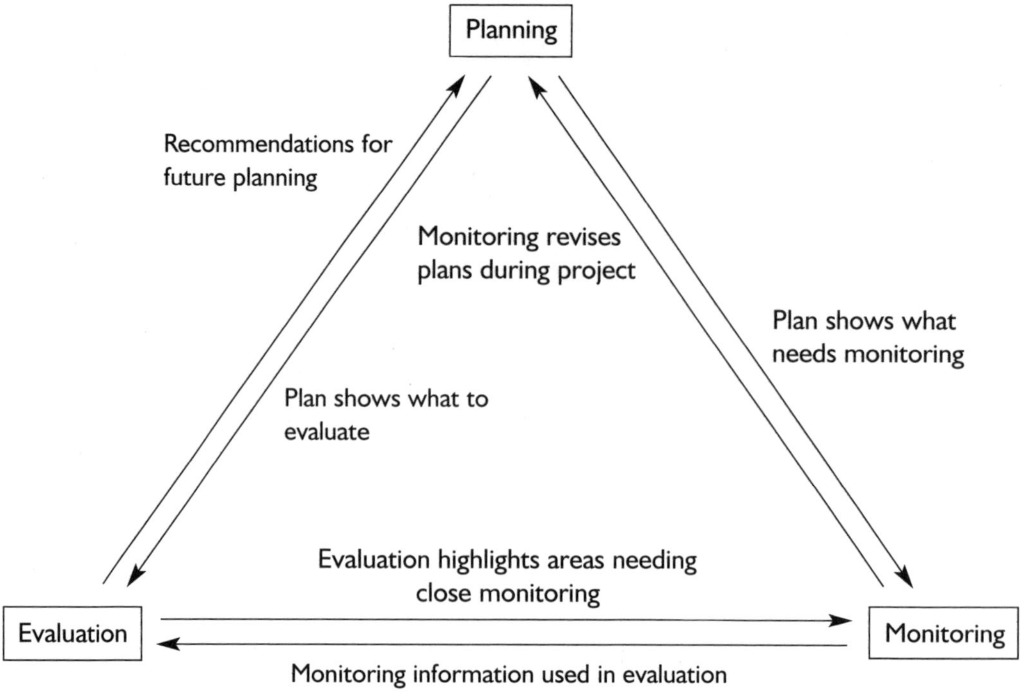

badly you will want to change them. Therefore, monitoring must influence the ongoing planning of the project. You will also see how far the project is keeping to the original objectives you set out to achieve and you may find that these objectives are moving as the project progresses. Therefore, monitoring will also influence how you evaluate the project's achievements.

When you come to evaluate the project, you will need to know what you originally set out to do and what has happened throughout the project. The former should be clear from the project plan. The latter should be available from the work you have done in monitoring. Evaluation is made much easier (many would say it is only possible) if the required information is collected during monitoring. Evaluating your activity may be very interesting and show that you have achieved very positive results, or it may show where things have gone wrong. In either case, it is useless if it does not influence the future planning for any development of the project or similar projects elsewhere.

These relationships are summarised in Figure 2. The three elements of planning, monitoring and evaluation are intimately linked and cannot be dealt with in isolation. When put together as a triangle they can serve as the basis for a strong project, but if one element is missing the resulting project is likely to be weak, like a triangle which is missing one corner. The whole project will become even stronger as there is a process of feedback between planning, monitoring and evaluation – this can be represented by the smaller triangles in Figure 2.

Project Cycle

Before moving on to discuss monitoring and evaluation in greater detail, it is important to present some of the common ideas and terminology used in project management. The

Figure 3: *The project cycle*

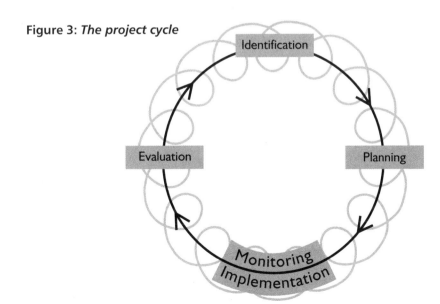

origins of each social development project or programme lie in the identification of a problem which it is thought an organisation can address through its intervention. The following steps of planning, implementation, monitoring and evaluation are often simplistically represented by the project cycle (see Figure 3) in which evaluation leads to identification of further projects. The grey spiral gives a more realistic representation as there will be a continuous interaction between all elements of the project cycle – in practice things do not move smoothly from identification, to planning, to implementation etc., as a plain circle suggests. The project cycle and issues of project identification and planning are covered in greater detail in other books (e.g. Gosling and Edwards 1995, Mikkelsen 1995) and may well be familiar to many readers, who may be tempted to move quickly over this section. However, since different organisations use different terms, it is important to cover some of this ground in this guide.

The project plan should make clear the link between the problem and how the planned activities are expected to contribute to a solution. These links are often described by breaking down the project into different levels: goals, objectives, outputs and activities.

At the top level is the overall goal to which the project hopes to make a significant contribution by achieving its objectives, the next level down. These objectives represent results which the project hopes to bring about. The objectives are further broken down into outputs which are smaller results which the project can be confident of producing. These outputs are produced by a set of activities which are undertaken by the project stakeholders.

Example – drawn from a mother and child community health project

Goal	reduce under 5 mortality by 20% in 3 years [the project will contribute to this aim, but many other factors, such as food production, will also influence infant mortality] *Learn*
Objective	within 3 years, 90% of families in district will have access to a mother and child health worker each month [this is directly related to the project but may depend on some factors beyond its control, such as newly trained health workers taking up jobs]
Output	6 new mother and child health workers trained by the end of year 1 [responsibility for this output should lie directly within the management of the project]
Activities	run 2 one-week training courses for MCH workers

Some organisations use different terms for these different levels:

Level	Alternative terms
Goal	Aim, General objective, Super-goal
Objective	Purpose, Outcome, Specific objective
Output	Results

Logical Framework

This hierarchy of objectives may be presented in a project matrix (often called a logical framework) which summarises the logic explaining how the activities are expected to contribute to the overall goal (see Table 2). Many donors require a logical framework to be developed before they will consider funding a project.

The logical framework approach has three major advantages[8]:

- It ensures that the project plan does work out how the activities undertaken in the project do relate to helping improve the problem the project is addressing.

- It requires the plan to consider how the progress of the project and its success (or failure) will be demonstrated.

- By listing assumptions and risks, it takes into account external factors beyond the project's control which might affect its progress.

However, it also has disadvantages which are worth outlining here:

- The preparation of a logical framework often becomes an exercise in filling in boxes, which is carried out to keep donors happy.

- Once it is in place, it can become a rigid document, which locks the projects into a particular path rather than evolving in the light of events and experience.

- The layout and the way it is used tends to put more emphasis on numerical measures of progress rather than more descriptive measures; this makes it less useful for tracking social change and impact.

- As a summary of the project, it can ignore the unexpected results and consequences of the project.

- It is a weak tool for the monitoring and evaluation of impact as the actual impacts of a project are often not included within the logical framework. It is much better for the monitoring and evaluation of outputs and outcomes.

Some of these disadvantages can be minimised if a participatory approach to project planning is adopted so all stakeholders are involved in developing the logical framework and it is regularly revised through participatory reviews.

---

[8] See Cracknell (2000:108–17) for a detailed discussion of the logical framework.

Table 2: *Project matrix or logical framework* (Adapted from Mikkelsen 1995: 51)

Narrative summary	Objectively verifiable indicators	Means of verification	Assumptions
Goal – the overall aim to which the project is expected to contribute.	Measures (direct or indirect) to show the project's contribution to the goal.	Sources of information and methods used to show fulfillment of goal.	Important events, conditions or decisions beyond the project's control necessary for maintaining the progress towards the goal.
Objectives – the new situation which the project is aiming to bring about.	Measures (direct or indirect) to show what progress is being made towards reaching the objectives.	Sources of information and methods used to show progress against objectives.	Important events, conditions or decisions beyond the project's control, which are necessary if achieving the objectives is going to contribute towards the overall goal.
Outputs – the results which should be within the control of the project management.	Measures (direct or indirect) to show if project outputs are being delivered.	Sources of information and methods used to show delivery of outputs.	Important events, conditions or decisions beyond the project's control, which are necessary if producing the outputs is going to help achieve the objectives.
Activities – the things which have to be done by the project to produce the outputs.	Measures (direct or indirect) to show if project outputs are being delivered.	Sources of information and methods used to show that activities have been completed.	Important events, conditions or decisions beyond the project's control, which are necessary if completing activities will produce the required outputs.
Inputs.	Resources – type and level of resources needed for the project. Finance – overall budget. Time – planned start and end date.		

Despite the disadvantages, the logical framework approach can be helpful for developing a monitoring and evaluation system. First, the different levels of goals, objectives and outputs are useful levels for monitoring and evaluation. Second, the logical framework introduces indicators to the project plan and these are a vital element of the monitoring and evaluation system.

Levels of Monitoring and Evaluation:
Outputs, Outcomes and Impact

One of the key issues for a monitoring and evaluation system is to establish what needs to be monitored and evaluated. Using the community health project example given above (page 16), if we assess the number of health workers trained and it matches our project plan, we may want to say the project has been successful. However, if the government has not provided the funds to pay those health workers as it promised, the objective of improving people's access to health workers will not have been met. Those newly trained health workers may then go and work in another district instead and bring an improvement in health services there. In terms of its original plan, the project will have failed, but it may have brought unintended benefits elsewhere. The job of assessing what a project has actually achieved is rarely as straightforward as the project framework might suggest.

There are three levels of results of a project which need to be distinguished:

- **Outputs** – the tangible products which are delivered on the completion of the project activities. **What was done?**

- **Outcomes** – the immediate and observable change, in relation to the project objectives, which is brought about as a direct result of project activities and the delivery of outputs. **What happened?**

- **Impact** – impact concerns long-term and sustainable changes introduced by a given intervention in the lives of stakeholders. Impact can be related either to the specific objectives of an intervention or to unanticipated changes caused by an intervention; such unanticipated changes may also occur in the lives of people who were not expected to be affected by the project. Impact can be either positive or negative – both are equally important.[9] **What changed?**

It is possible to monitor and evaluate a project's progress at each of these levels and each is measuring something different (see Table 3):

---

[9] Adapted from Blankenberg (1995).

- If we look at outputs, we are seeing how much work has been done by the project – the **effort** put in.

- Measuring outcomes is concerned with seeing what immediate **effect** the project has had on the initial situation. This is more than the total effort put into the project but what actually happens as a result of those efforts. It will therefore need to take into account the way that the project beneficiaries have actually received whatever benefits the project is aiming to bring.

- Measuring impact is hardest of all as it is looking at the longer-term **change** brought about as a result of the project. This must take into account other factors external to the project, which have interacted with it. They may make it very difficult to be sure that the changes described are actually arising from the project rather than these other factors.

Table 3: *Different levels for monitoring and evaluation*
(adapted from Fowler 1997: 164)

Point of measurement	What is measured	Indicators
Outputs	Effort	Implementation of activities
Outcomes	Effect	Use of outputs and sustained production of benefits
Impact	Change	Difference from the original situation

The focus of many monitoring and evaluation systems is at the first point of measurement, outputs, and much of the project reporting takes place at this level. This shows how well the project is delivering on its outputs but it often says little about the change (positive or negative) brought about by the project.

Assessing impact is more complex. It is not represented by numerical indicators which allow for simple measurement, but must usually be described as a qualitative change. It requires consideration of a wide range of factors many of which may lie outside the project. It occurs slowly over a long time period and may not easily be captured within the normal round of quarterly and annual reporting. Positive and negative impacts may occur at different stages. For example, a women's literacy project may have the positive impact of increasing participants' job opportunities and income. However, in time, this may change the gender relations within households and result in a reaction by men engaging in more domestic violence.

Linking the Project's Activities and its Impact

Monitoring and evaluation cannot be expected to prove the link between the project activities and the described impact, but they should present a convincing case for an association between the cause and effect. Projects are not scientific experiments and they are not carried out in laboratories. It is not possible to provide irrefutable scientific proof that long-term changes occur as a direct result of the project activities (with the corollary that if the project had *not* taken place the change would certainly not have occurred). There are so many other factors involved that it is always difficult to work out the links of cause and effect.

For example, a project may aim to increase agricultural production by providing loans for farm inputs. It may observe that production does steadily increase during the project. However, it is difficult to prove that this increase is a result of the loans rather than other factors – for instance, if the market prices for crops increase, this may also stimulate greater production.

Even where the case can be made for linking the project to impact, this will not necessarily be a clear guide for action. The intervening factors must be taken into account. In the example of the women's literacy class, given above, teaching women to read can be linked to an increase in domestic violence. However, it would be dangerous and wrong to claim that increasing women's literacy *causes* domestic violence – the violence is caused by men choosing to react with their fists or feet. It is important to understand the impact that the project is having in order to know how to respond to it (e.g. working with the men, conflict management initiatives etc.), but it may be wrong to claim that the project is *responsible* for the negative impact.

Many projects make great claims of their results with little evidence. The monitoring and evaluation system is expected to provide evidence that the project has caused a set of immediate effects and long-term changes. The system must be able to show that this evidence is both credible and valid.

Introduction to Indicators

Indicators are a very important element of a monitoring and evaluation system. In this context, an indicator is an observable change or event which provides evidence that something has happened – whether an output delivered, immediate effect occurred or long-term change observed. They do not provide proof so much as reliable signs that the event or process being claimed has actually happened (or is happening). The evidence from a number of indicators will provide the convincing case for the claims being made.

One of the very useful parts of the logical framework approach is that it forces those planning the project to show indicators at each level – indicators of effort, effect and change. These indicators provide a very good base for the monitoring and evaluation system.

In the case of some activities and concrete outputs, the indicators of effort may simply be observing that an event has taken place or an output has been delivered – for example:

Output	Indicator
100 km of rural road built within first year	Numbers of kilometres of road completed at end of first year

Such outputs may be further qualified – e.g. setting technical standards for road building which must be met. However, some outputs are not so easily visible and quantifiable and it may be necessary to use more descriptive indicators to show that the output has been delivered. Such descriptive indicators are usually the most appropriate for assessing a social development project's effects and its impact – for example:

Objective	Indicators
Greater participation of women co-operative members in decision making	Increase in number of women elected as officials Women members initiate new co-operative activities

It is very important not to confuse the indicators with the outputs, objectives or goal. Achieving the expected change in the indicators should not become the primary target of the project. There may be many reasons why the indicators do not change as planned, but this does not mean that the project is failing. It may simply show that the indicators are inappropriate. The focus should always be on what the indicators are pointing to rather than the indicators themselves. This is important to ensure that the project does not become trapped in a cycle of chasing movements in indicators, rather than the social change which it set out to achieve.

There are many different types of indicators and they need to be carefully chosen to ensure that the monitoring and evaluation system provides the required information at an appropriate cost. The most basic division is between quantitative and qualitative indicators:

Quantitative – where the change in the indicators can be shown through numbers – e.g. the number of people attending clinics.

Qualitative – where the change in the indicators is shown through description – e.g. the level of responsibility of a village development committee.

Whichever sort of indicator is used it should be:

- **Specific** – clearly related to areas in which the project is expected to make a difference;

- **Unambiguous** – clearly defined so that all stakeholders can agree on their measurement and interpretation;

- **Credible** – it is reasonable to claim that changes in the indicators are related, either directly or indirectly, to the project intervention;

- **Consistent** – the main body of indicators remains the same and they are measured over a long time;

- **Easy to collect** – it must be feasible to collect information on the chosen indicators within a reasonable time and at a reasonable cost.

As noted above, indicators are a vital component of the monitoring and evaluation system and this is only a brief introduction to them. These and other issues are discussed in greater detail in Chapter 5 in Part 2.

Baselines

Ideally the analysis of the problem which the project is aiming to address will provide a clear picture of the initial situation, or baseline. However, often this is not the case and as the project is planned and objectives and outputs are defined, it will be necessary to carry out a baseline study to describe fully the current situation. As the project is implemented things will change, and by comparing the new situation to the baseline, it will be possible to assess what progress has been made.

For example, if a project aims to address chronic malnutrition by increasing household food production for project beneficiaries, it will need to know how much food is being produced before the project starts.

In preparing a baseline study the following issues should be considered:

- Build in participation and learning so the baseline study is not simply gathering information for the project, but can also be part of a process of local communities finding out and analysing their situation. Involving project beneficiaries at this stage will help them to understand what the project is doing and to monitor its progress.

- The views of different stakeholders should be taken into account as they may have different views of the current situation – e.g. male village leaders may say that women participate fully in village decisions through the women's representative, many women may say that they have influence through their husbands, whereas NGO staff from the community may see that women are excluded from decision making.

- The cost (in money, time, human and other resources) to obtain and analyse the information.

- The need to limit the scope of the baseline study and the number of questions asked – it is important to find a balance between the requirement for sufficient detail, with the cost of getting it.

Optimum ignorance

- The baseline situation will change even without the project intervention
  – so do not waste resources obtaining detailed information about factors which are likely to face large changes due to events outside the project's control.

A basic checklist for designing a baseline study

- Identify stakeholders
- What is the main reason for doing this study?
- What questions do you want to be able to answer later?
- Hence, what questions do you want to be able to answer now?
- What evidence would be needed to answer these questions?
- Who/where would you get this evidence from? (sources of information)
- What methods would you use?
- Who would do the work?
- What resources are required?
- What is the time scale?

In some projects, it may be more appropriate to establish a baseline by monitoring the situation of potential participants in the project before they join its activities. This may be appropriate for projects that are expected to expand their coverage to new areas or to new individuals. By comparing the situation of those already involved in the project with those who are yet to take part, it is possible to assess how far the project is making a difference in the lives of participants.

This approach has the advantage of providing a 'moving baseline' which will reflect changes in the wider context, in which the project is operating. For example, if the economy starts to grow rapidly, the changes visible from an 'historical baseline', which was established at a set time in the past, may be very dramatic but not necessarily related to the project. The differences between the situation of the project beneficiaries and the 'moving baseline' may be more moderate as the current situation of potential participants will reflect the changes in the economic situation.

Figure 4: *Historical versus 'moving' baselines*

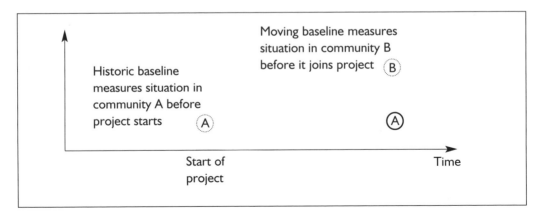

CHAPTER 2

Monitoring

Recall the definition of monitoring introduced in the previous chapter:

> **Monitoring** is the systematic and continuous assessment of the progress of a piece of work over time, which checks that things are 'going to plan' and enables adjustments to made in a methodical way.

If we consider the monitoring and evaluation system as a building, monitoring is the foundation on which everything else rests. It may be less prominent than evaluation, and at times less interesting, but without proper monitoring of the project, sound evaluation will be impossible. Without monitoring, an evaluation exercise may be carried out, but its findings will be shaky and liable to collapse – like a wall with no foundation.

Various definitions of monitoring can be found in different books[1] but they all suggest that monitoring *must* be:

(a) an integral part of project management at all levels; and

(b) a structured and continuous process for collecting, storing, analysing and using data and information and not something which is done periodically in an *ad hoc* manner.

Even if a formal monitoring system is not yet established, those involved in the project from day to day, especially at the field level, will inevitably be engaged in monitoring its progress as a matter of course. This may take the form of filling in daily report forms or field diaries. It may also include filing information such as press reports or photographs of events within the project. In a recent study of NGOs in Ethiopia, it was found that *no* junior staff saw these activities as part of the monitoring system. Instead, they perceived monitoring as a sophisticated and technical set of activities from which they were excluded by their junior position.[2]

It is therefore very important that field staff are fully involved in the development of the monitoring system and it is not perceived as a tool of senior management imposed from on high. A new monitoring system should not displace existing monitoring activities but build on them.

---

[1] See bibliography.
[2] Mebrahtu (2003).

Too often monitoring becomes a routine exercise of collecting information to keep management or donors happy, but it offers little to help the progress of the project at the field level. Data is collected and then simply passed on to those who need it. Information on impact is rarely gathered as part of a monitoring system and it is left to evaluations to uncover the impact at the end of the project – when it may be too late to change things for the better. This approach to monitoring is inadequate as for most people involved, especially at the field level; it is not worth going to the effort of collecting information if it is not analysed, discussed and reflected upon at different levels. Such a monitoring system will fall into disuse as people will do the bare minimum required to satisfy management or the donors.

This should not be the case with a participatory monitoring system. In designing the monitoring system it is important to balance the interests of the various stakeholders.

For example:

- *The local community* may want to monitor the impact of the project – what do they see happening as a result of the project?

- *Project staff* may want to see if the project is making progress against the objectives – are they achieving what they set out to do?

- *Donors* may be very interested regularly to see progress against the outputs – is the money they are giving being used as proposed?

Many donors will request a regular report on a project or programme that they are funding – at least annually, possibly twice a year, and sometimes quarterly. As a result, monitoring systems are often biased towards producing the reports which donors require and neglect the interests of other stakeholders, particularly the local community. Ideally a well designed monitoring system will provide the information and analysis for donor reports at the same time as enabling the local community to assess the project's progress.

Establishing a Monitoring System

It is important to plan how you will monitor the work before the project starts. It may seem premature to start worrying about how you assess what you have done, before you have done anything, but if you do not set up a monitoring system from the start you will find it more difficult to do it later. As far as possible a monitoring system should be put in place before the project starts, so that it can operate from the beginning of the project's activities. The following issues will need to be decided when setting up a monitoring system:

What Information Should be Used?
Discuss with stakeholders who needs what information and select appropriate indicators (the selection of indicators is discussed in greater detail in Chapter 5). This needs to be a

participatory process as different stakeholders may have very different ideas of what observable changes will result from the project's activities. Initially a very long list of indicators may be suggested but it is vital that a manageable number is used if the process of monitoring is not to become too time consuming.

The set of indicators should include those which can measure effort, effect and change in order to assess the delivery of outputs, the achievement of planned outcomes and the project's impact. As far as possible it is important to try to select indicators which can be monitored over the course of the project. However, it will not be possible to determine all the appropriate indicators before the project starts and the monitoring system must be flexible enough to cope with changes. Indicators may stop being useful for a number of reasons:

- The information is too difficult to collect or unreliable;

- Other events cause much larger changes to the indicator than any result of the project's work;

- There is no discernible change in the indicator over time – this may suggest that the project is not having the anticipated effect (in which case the lack of change is evidence of a problem with the project) or that the relationship between the project activities and the indicator is not valid. In the latter case the indicator is inappropriate.

Other indicators may emerge during the course of the project as unexpected results are observed. As these arise they should be included in the monitoring system. For example, a project which improves health conditions may result in a labour surplus as few days are lost to sickness or funerals.

Who Will Collect the Information?

It may be appropriate for different people to gather different information, depending on the source of data and the method of collection.

- Project staff – is there a potential for bias as they clearly have an interest in ensuring that that their performance is seen in a good light? Will there be a tendency for people to tell project staff what they want to hear?

- Project participants – also liable to bias as they have an interest in continuing to receive the project benefits for themselves. They may have limited capacity for some forms of data collection.

- Community leaders – would community members have time and interest to continue collecting information after the initial enthusiasm wears off? If the work is likely to involve considerable effort, it may be necessary to think about how people will be compensated for it. It is important not to have unrealistic expectation of what people will volunteer to do.

© Bill Crooks 2003

How Will Monitoring Information be Collected?

There are wide range of different tools for collecting monitoring information, including interviews with individuals and groups, formal surveys, participatory rapid appraisal and observation. The choice of appropriate methods will depend on various factors such as the nature of the project, the skills of the staff and project participants, the timescale for the project, and the resources available. See Chapter 6 for more details on these methods and the criteria for selecting the most appropriate.

When choosing data collection methods, it is important to bear in mind that monitoring is an ongoing process and you must plan for repeated data collection. For example, if you decide to use regular surveys or other regular interviews, you must also consider who you will be asking each time. If the same people are likely to be asked over the time of the project, in order to identify changes in their situation, it may be necessary to look for volunteers who will be prepared to answer questions repeatedly.

When Will Information be Collected?

It is important to be realistic and not to collect data too frequently, as this will result in people finding it too much of a burden and losing interest. It will also mean that it is impossible to keep up with the analysis. The timing of data collection will depend on the type of data and the methods of data collection. Filling in a form to report how many people attended a weekly class sounds sensible, but interviewing class members each week about the difference the classes are making to their lives would probably be excessive.

It is often more appropriate to collect data on indicators of effort more frequently than that on indicators of change. Social change takes time and looking at the situation too frequently may actually make it harder to perceive changes. In the same way, it is difficult for parents to see the growth of their children because they see them every day, but visitors who see them less frequently will easily see the change over time. The appropriate timing for data collection will only become clear with experience.

Who Will Organise and Analyse Monitoring Information?

It is most likely to be project staff who have the resources to organise and analyse data and they may also be the most interested. There will almost inevitably be some sort of hierarchy of reports, especially within an organisation which is involved in more than one project. Field staff responsible for one project will pass reports on to senior staff who will draw together a summary from reports for a number of projects (see below).

It needs to be made clear to people where monitoring information will end up and in particular who will be receiving the project reports. It is easy to share positive reports widely, but if there are problems it is important that they are handled sensitively. In deciding where reports should be circulated the following issues should be considered:

- Some people may be enemies of the project – especially if it undermines their interests, and they may take up any negative comments in a report to attack the work. For example, if the project aims to increase people's access to piped water, it may damage the livelihoods of water sellers who transport clean water into the community.

- Writing for public consumption may make the process of report writing more difficult and time consuming.

- Much depends on how reports are treated – are they used as learning documents or as sticks with which to beat project staff? If the latter, it will be in the interests of project staff to prevent problems and difficulties appearing in the reports.

- There is always a problem of trust where different people have different interests. The only way round it is to make sure that there is a good rapport between the project users, project staff and other stakeholders.

- It will be important to strike the balance between accountability (downwards and upwards) and enabling the project to report on its mistakes and learn from them.

How Will the Findings from Monitoring be Used?

Apart from going into reports for donors, what other mechanisms will be established to make findings from monitoring influence the way the project is run? It may be appropriate to hold regular review meetings with local stakeholders such as project users, staff and other community representatives to discuss the progress of the project in the light of monitoring reports. Such meetings would be a good chance to present evidence about the project's progress, deal with particular issues arising and make plans for the future. It may also be possible to issue a report locally in the form of a newsletter to advise people of how things are going. If particular issues arise from monitoring it may be appropriate to bring together a special project workshop with other stakeholders to consider how these issues should be addressed.

Keeping the Momentum Going

A monitoring system is based on the regular collection of data and this will only continue if those collecting the data see it that it is worthwhile and useful. The exception might be project staff who will continue to collect data as part of their jobs, but the quality of the information will go down if they do not see the point of it. This does not mean that data has to be used immediately – e.g. information on trends is only likely to be useful after a number of observations have been made so that a trend can emerge – but the reason for wanting it must be clear.

It is therefore critical that the data collected in the monitoring system is seen to be useful by those who are collecting it. This can be encouraged by developing a culture of regular reflection and analysis within the project, so that the data can be reviewed, progress assessed and changes made as required. However, it is also important to ensure that such times of reflection do not themselves become a burden to those involved in the project. It is only worth having meetings when there is something to discuss.

For example, a weekly progress meeting involving all staff and project clients for a project running for three years is likely to be frustrating and demoralising as very few changes will be noticeable from week to week. People will soon resent the time spent and stop coming. A quarterly review involving local project stakeholders can realistically expect to have something to report – and if it does not, then there is a problem to be addressed.

Setting up a System for Managing Data

A monitoring system can very rapidly gather a large amount of information and it is essential that this is recorded and stored in a way which makes it available for later review and analysis – possibly during an evaluation. This can be quite straightforward in the case of numerical information, which can be regularly recorded on standard forms and filed in date order. (See Box 6 for an example.)

However, monitoring social development projects inevitably involves the tracking of social changes, which tends to depend on qualitative data. The real challenge is capturing qualitative information in a useful way. On reviewing many projects, it often becomes clear

Box 6: *Monitoring systems case study* *(Marsden et al. (1994): 76–82)*

CINDE, Colombia

Over some years the International Centre for Education and Human Development, CINDE, has been implementing community-based approaches to early childhood care and education. The programme began by encouraging groups of mothers from the poorest sections of the communities to stimulate the development of their pre-school children by playing games with them in the home. During the meetings, the mothers started to identify other problems related to topics such as health, nutrition and income generation. Over time the project evolved into an integrated community development project addressing such issues. Despite the poverty of the area in which the programme operates, the focus of the work has been on educational and organisational processes. The work has been led in each community by a *promotora*, or facilitator, many of whom are mothers from the poorest sectors of the community. These *promotoras* have been the main educational agents in the programme.

From the outset the parents have been involved in the management of the programme. Monitoring and evaluation have been an integral part of the programme, not only to improve and assess the work, but also as a fundamental strategy to build the capacity of the individual participants and the communities. The monitoring system uses various approaches including:

- *Reporting and recording meetings* – each group keeps an individual record or log-book which is prepared by the group. For example, at meetings with pre-school mothers a point is made of evaluating the work done by each mother since the last encounter and how it has affected the development of her children. In the nutrition programme, the children are weighed and measured each week and a simple graph is developed by the mothers so that they can see the progress made. The group discusses the records reflecting on why there has been an improvement or decline in the results.

  In addition, the *promotoras* and CINDE staff write reports on activities in which they note their observations with respect to the objectives, achievements and any difficulties faced.

- *Survey/diagnosis/questionnaire* – undertaken by the community to evaluate situation before the programmes start – often based on mapping. For example, at the start of a campaign for the installation of latrines the community developed a map, locating the houses with latrines and those without latrines, and showing the altitude of the different parts of the community to indicate the possibility of underground septic tanks. This helps stimulate the community to visualise the problem, locating the areas where the problem is more severe, and creates a basis against which to monitor their progress.

- *Group discussions* – meetings and activities are evaluated through group discussions which provide an opportunity to discuss the collective views on activities and the changes which seem to be occurring.

- *Key informants* – individual discussions with one or two *promotoras* or community leaders are used as a way of monitoring developments and checking the validity of previous findings.

- *Workshops* – at least once a year, workshops are organised with the *promotoras* and CINDE staff to analyse development, to check the project is on course and to make necessary changes.

These different approaches serve to help the community reflect and visualise their problem and to stimulate and motivate them to continue with activities or develop new actions. Moreover they serve as a form of continuous monitoring of project activities.

that the project users and staff have a very good idea of what is happening, where the project is achieving its aims and where there are problems. They will relate stories and events which illustrate wider points about the project. They may not have analysed these to draw out project lessons – it may remain at the level of 'this is how they do things here, we don't really understand why it is like that, but it is, and we go along with it'. A monitoring system should as far as possible aim to pick up this sense of what is happening.

Although some monitoring activities should be helpful in themselves – for example, holding a review meeting with local stakeholders – it is vitally important that a record is made of these events and stored. By looking at these records at later stages, it will be possible to assess changes over time and they will provide a base of information for evaluation. This information will be the main source of evidence for claims about the project's effect and impact. Ideally the monitoring system should allow a chain of evidence to be established that links the project's impact to its activities and the delivery of outputs.

Although information gathering should involve a range of stakeholders, it is most likely that the responsibility for record keeping will lie with project staff. The records for the monitoring system are likely to include the following:

- Report forms: standardised forms which record regularly occurring data, especially quantitative data, e.g. number of people attending meetings, market prices.

- Meeting reports: minutes of routine meetings, such as staff meetings, project management committee meetings, project review meetings.

- Visit reports: records of routine field visits by project staff.

- Monitoring exercise records: depending on the data and the method of data collection (see Chapter 6), there may be particular monitoring exercises such as surveys or interviews which take place.

- Staff diaries: notebooks recording particular events, comments and other details about the project which are not included in the other parts of the monitoring system – these might be one way of picking up unintended effects of the project.

- Other information relating to the project: photographs, press-cuttings.

Each record should include the date it was written and the name of the person preparing it.

It is important that these basic records are kept short and concise, so that they can be reread with the minimum of effort. This can be a great challenge for qualitative data. A critical issue is how to strike the balance between generating too much or too little description. The former can be overwhelming and the later insufficient for drawing conclusions as to outcome and impact. In this matter there are no universal rules. Experience gained through trial and error will help in determining the minimum but realistic amount of description, taking into account factors such as staff time, availability and cost-effectiveness, which would produce adequate evidence for the purposes of evaluation. It is important that the volume of information required by the system is restricted. A minimum but effective system has more chance of actually functioning than a demanding and information-hungry one.

If the organisation is large and involves a number of different projects or programmes, it may be helpful to develop a more formal system with a standard format for basic monitoring records. Each record could summarise the following information on not more than one side of A4 paper:

- Tool/Instrument – What method was used to collect information?

- Source – Who provided the information? – name of interviewee, type of interviewee, number in group etc.

- Date – When was the tool used? – date or range of dates if used over a period (e.g. weekly diary may have been used between 1/5/03-30/6/03)

- Relevant indicators – What indicators was information gathered on?

- Results – For each relevant indicator, what did the monitoring process show about the indicator? Make sure that you include negative or no change results as well as positive changes in the indicators.

- Other observations – Any other observations or results which show some evidence of progress in meeting the objectives but which are not included in the list of indicators.

In addition in order to help establish the chain of evidence and make cross referencing easier, each record should show which project or programme collected the data and also have a unique reference which will allow cross referencing to this piece of data at every level of the organisation. For example this could take the form Year/Region/project/consecutive no. e.g. 02/S/CD/4.

This data should be summarised in a basic monitoring record sheet. A possible format is shown in Figure 5. There should be a separate record for each use of monitoring tools. This basic record should not take up more than one side of A4 paper. These basic monitoring record sheets will form the basis for regular monitoring reports – most likely monthly or quarterly depending on the project. These reports will draw together the results of the various monitoring exercises carried out over the previous period, present them in summary form and include some analysis of the findings.

Figure 5: *Basic monitoring record sheet*
This is a summary record for any monitoring activity. It should not take more than one page

Unique Reference:	Project:	Date:
Tool:		
Source:		
Indicator	**Result**	
Indicator 1 – only include indicators for which you have information in this record	The result (positive or negative) relating to the indicator which was shown through this tool	
Indicator 2	...	
Indicator 3	...	
...	...	
...	...	
...	...	
Other observations: Any other observations which you think demonstrate progress in meeting objectives but which are not included in the list of indicators		

Figure 6: *Project monitoring report*

Unique Reference:		Project:		Date:

Source: Unique references for data sources for report

Overall objective	Level	Indicators	Result
Objective 1	Effort	Effort indicator 1 Effort indicator 2	Summary of the results (positive or negative) given in basic monitoring records relating to the indicator
	Effect	Effect indicator 1 Effect indicator 2	...
	Change	Change indicator 1 Change indicator 2	...
Objective 2	Effort	Effort indicator 1 Effort indicator 2	...
	Effect	Effect indicator 1 Effect indicator 2	...
	Change	Change indicator 1 Change indicator 2	...
Objective ...	Effort	Effort indicator 1 Effort indicator 2	...
	Effect	Effect indicator 1 Effect indicator 2	...
	Change	Change indicator 1 Change indicator 2	...
Other observations		Any other observations which you think demonstrate progress in meeting objectives but which are not included in the list of indicators	

Summary of results – this should show the progress made against each of the indicators which are relevant to the project. This can be presented as a table (see Figure 6 for a suggested format).

Analysis   what progress has been made during the last period?
             are there areas of concern where progress is behind?
             are there external changes effecting the project participants?
             are indicators appropriate and helpful?
             are appropriate methods being used to get data?

Issues arising   recommendations for changes in implementation
                 suggested changes to monitoring systems, e.g. new indicators

Ideally this sort of report should take no more than two sides of A4.

Figure 7: *Reporting Pyramid*

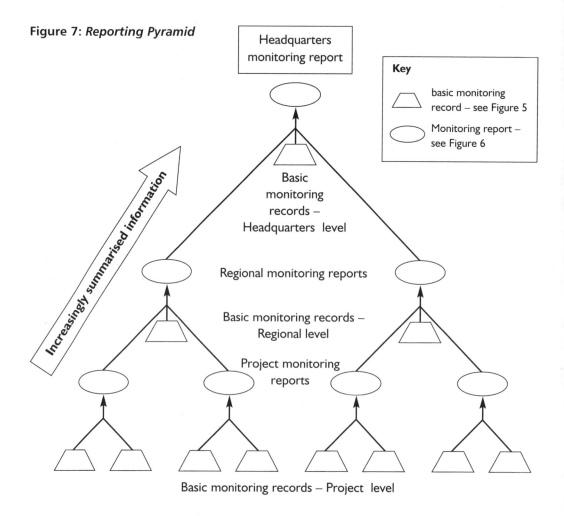

The majority of monitoring data will inevitably be collected in the field but some monitoring will also take place at any supporting offices, such as regional offices or an organisation's headquarters. This is important as the progress of a project is not just dependent on the activities and performance of project staff and users in the field, but it also relies on efficient administrative or other support from the organisation managing the project. For example, a donor is likely to provide funds through the main office and it will be essential that it manages the money well to ensure that there is sufficient flow of cash to the field. Depending on the circumstances, in a remote area supplies may be purchased through the head office in the city and problems with the logistics system will slow down the project's progress.

As reports are sent further from the field, the information in them tends to become more summarised as it is merged with data from other fields. At each stage those compiling the reports should be analysing both the data they produce at their own level and that which they receive from other levels and summarising it. As part of the process of summarising information, some data is left out. This is essential to ensure that as reports move from the field they do not become overloaded with detail; such reports will remain unread.

This process can be represented as a reporting pyramid (Figure 7). Monitoring data should never simply be passed from one level to the next without further analysis or adding new information. If any level has nothing to contribute to monitoring the progress other than receiving data from lower down the pyramid, this would suggest that that office has contributed nothing towards the project's objectives, i.e. it adds no value.

Using Monitoring Information for Decision Making

If monitoring information is simply gathered into reports for reference during a later evaluation, it will hardly justify the time and effort put into collecting it. The day to day lessons revealed by monitoring must be used for decision making, as they come to light. If monitoring shows that the project may be going off course, it is much better to pick up the problem early before things have gone too far adrift.

To this end it is very important that the organisation responds to the issues which are raised in the monitoring reports. These may require immediate action, further observation, or be able to wait until an evaluation or end of year review. The critical point is that a decision is taken about which response is required rather than leaving the issues lying in reports unread. Using data from monitoring and evaluation is discussed in more detail in Chapter 8.

CHAPTER 3
Evaluation

Evaluation is the periodic assessment of the relevance, performance, efficiency and impact of a piece of work with respect to its stated objectives. An evaluation is usually carried out at some significant stage in the project's development, e.g. at the end of a planning period, as the project moves to a new phase, or in response to a particular critical issue.

An evaluation will assess the progress which is being made towards achieving the project's overall objectives and its impact. This is never as straightforward as a first glance at a project framework might suggest. The planned links, described in the project framework, between the project's activities, outputs, objectives and goal will always be subject to changes within the project and the environment in which it operates. Some of the difficulties may have been included in the risks and assumptions for the project, but inevitably in practice new things will come up which were not anticipated.

Our understanding of evaluation in this guide is that it will focus more on the outcomes and impacts of the project rather than its outputs – these should be recorded and assessed through the monitoring system. If the monitoring system is not working properly, an evaluation may have to need to look at some details of the project activities and outputs. Some other definitions of evaluation restrict the focus more closely to assessing progress towards reaching objectives, leaving impact to be assessed in a separate exercise – an impact assessment. This is recognising that it is difficult to understand the impact of a project in the relatively short time frame of an evaluation. This will be true if data on the project's impact is not collected through monitoring. Once again we must stress the point made at the beginning of the in the previous chapter – *monitoring is the foundation on which evaluation is built.*

This chapter focuses on the practicalities of organising an evaluation. More details about data collection and analysis are given in Part 2.

Scope of Evaluation

It is very important to be clear about the scope of an evaluation – what is it that is to be evaluated? Limits must be set on what an evaluation should look at, to ensure that the exercise does not spiral out of control and absorb a huge amount of time, effort and money in assessing every aspect of work. An evaluation which does not start off with a clear focus is likely to produce a fuzzy report and fuzzy recommendations. These will not satisfy any stakeholders.

Evaluations may focus on many different aspects of the work but they can usually be described as evaluations of a project, programme, sector, strategy or relationship:

- *Project* – the evaluation focuses on the work of one project and only looks at wider strategic issues or other areas in as far as they relate to the project being evaluated.

- *Programme* – the evaluation looks at a range of projects which have been grouped together as a programme in a particular geographical area or engaged in a particular sector of work.

- *Sector* – an organisation involved in a number of projects in the same sector may want to evaluate all their activities in this sector, e.g. all income generating projects. This might also be described as a thematic evaluation or meta-evaluation.

- *Strategy* – an NGO may have adopted a particular strategy to address its overall organisational goals such as working in a particular region, focusing on a sector, adopting a particular approach to its work. It is important to evaluate the strategy to assess how far it is moving both the NGO and its stakeholders in an appropriate direction.

- *Relationships* – social development involves many different relationships and the quality of these relationships will have a strong influence on the effect and impact of development interventions. An evaluation may focus on a particular relationship to assess whether it is working well and facilitating the development projects. For example, donors may establish 'partnerships' with NGOs they support but it is important to assess how far the NGOs relate to the donor as a partner, or as a contractor relating to a client. The nature of the relationship may make a critical difference to development projects as it will determine how the NGO responds to donor pressure; does it jump when the donor tells it to?

An evaluation may take a very different approach depending on its scope. If it is concerned with donor/NGO relationship, most of the effort is likely to be put into assessments at the donor and NGO offices, with less time spent engaging with individual projects and their beneficiaries. In contrast, a project evaluation should expect to spend a much larger proportion of its time in the project area. This book is primarily about the evaluation of projects or programmes, but the principles outlined here equally apply to evaluations with a different scope.

Purpose of Evaluation

As noted in Chapter 1, monitoring and evaluation are important for accountability, improving performance, learning and communication. The emphasis of any particular evaluation will depend on the nature of the project, the stakeholders who are the driving force behind the evaluation and the particular issues facing the project at the time of the evaluation.

- Evaluation should be used to derive lessons from a completed project, so that these may be used to guide future strategies.

- How the project will be evaluated should be considered during planning, and evaluation should be integrated into the design of projects; in addition, the lessons learned from evaluation should feed into future planning.

- Implementing agencies need information with which to compare the successes and failures of various activities they support and carry out.

- Donor agencies seek to ensure that their limited funds are directed towards worthwhile projects; evaluation can therefore be a means of clearly demonstrating the effectiveness of an intervention.

Whatever the purpose, it is essential that it is clear. Many NGOs are frustrated by the results of evaluations because the purpose was not entirely clear to the evaluators, hence they produce something that does not meet the needs of the client. The purpose for the evaluation will determine the methods and approaches used and the resources required. This is important to avoid undertaking an evaluation which does not meet the needs of any of the stakeholders, such as the donors, the NGO or the beneficiaries.

It is better to be honest about the purpose rather than shroud it in confusion. Thus if a heavy handed audit is required then this should be carried out, rather than trying to do a 'participatory' evaluation process, which is either dishonest or unable to produce the detailed financial information required for the audit. Conversely a technical financial audit is unlikely to show us much about the impact of the intervention or the perception of the intended beneficiaries of the intervention.

Evaluation Criteria

It is important to establish a framework for an evaluation so that those involved know what they are looking for in the evaluation. Whether the purpose of the evaluation is focused on accountability or learning, it will be concerned with making judgements about the project, programme or whatever is being evaluated. In order to do this it is essential to have some criteria against which to make the judgement. The specific details of the criteria will vary with each evaluation but they will usually fit within five broad areas: efficiency, effectiveness, impact, relevance and sustainability. These criteria have been adopted as a standard by the Development Assistance Committee of the Organisation for Economic Co-operation and Development (OECD) for assessing development aid and they are often used by donors when they are initiating evaluations.

Efficiency

This assesses the outputs in relation to the inputs to the project. It asks questions about whether the inputs have been used in the best way possible to produce the required outputs. Could other more efficient approaches have been used to the same end? Were the outputs delivered as required – both in quantity and quality (on time, in the right place etc.)?

Effectiveness

Effectiveness is concerned with how far delivering the project outputs actually achieved the desired outcome. Did all the effort have the expected effect? Could a stronger effect have been achieved through different outputs?

Impact

What changes have occurred as a result of the project, for individuals (distinguishing people by gender, age and ethnic groups as appropriate), communities, and institutions? This should include both changes relating to goals of the project and also unintended impacts which were not anticipated.

Relevance

The extent to which the project objectives and goals match the priorities and policies of the major stakeholders. Is the project concerned with problems which are important to people, particularly the intended beneficiaries, or could the project resources have been better used to address other issues? For example, a project which successfully improves market access may be of limited benefit if farmers do not produce a significant surplus to sell.

Sustainability

How far any changes brought about by the project are likely to continue in the longer term. This might be concerned about the continuation of project activities (e.g. community literacy classes), the durability of project outputs (e.g. the maintenance of a well), and the sustained impact of the project (e.g. improved access to healthcare). There are a number of aspects to sustainability, which should be considered:

- Financial – what will be the ongoing needs for funding at the end of the project and what sources of funding are available?

- Organisational – how will any future work in the project areas be organised? Who will manage it, who will control it, what will happen when individuals withdraw from it?

- Institutional – how far are changes in social practice likely to persist? Has the project contributed to new patterns of behaviour, social arrangements or routines which will be long lasting?

These different aspects are important whether we are assessing the sustainability of activities, outputs or impacts. Table 4 illustrates some of the questions which might be asked for different aspects of sustainability at different levels of project results.

Table 4: *Questions to assess aspects of sustainability at different levels of project results*

	Activities e.g. continuing literacy	**Outputs** e.g. well remains usable	**Impact** e.g. improved access to primary healthcare (PHC)
Financial sustainability	How will new teaching materials be paid for?	How will spare parts be purchased?	Is there a statutory budget for PHC services?
Organisational sustainability	Is the teacher willing to continue? Will the classroom still be available?	Who will purchase spare parts? How will decisions about the well be made?	Who is making decisions about PHC priorities? How accountable are PHC managers to local community?
Institutional sustainability	Will people continue to be committed to becoming literate?	Are people becoming used to clean water as a normal part of life – so they will challenge any obstacles to their access to it?	Are people referring to PHC services in preference to traditional medicine? Is government committed to principle of PHC?

Participatory and Conventional Evaluation

Evaluations are often commissioned by donors at a significant point in the project or programme – e.g. the end of the project or funding cycle, or as part of a strategic review. Their focus may be on accountability and the results of the evaluation may be used by the donors as a the basis for decisions about future funding. The criteria for evaluation are set in advance, often based on the indicators contained in the project framework. In the past, donors have preferred evaluations to be led by external consultants, whom they perceive to have a more 'objective' view of the programme.

Such conventional evaluations are often frustrated by a lack of hard quantitative and qualitative data and information at the project level. The conclusions rest too heavily on the experience, observations and judgement of the consultants. These results are objective only to the extent that they are based on the views of an external observer, but they are inevitably based on insufficient information and knowledge about the project. Although the external consultants may be used to avoiding the bias of those directly involved in the project, it is also important to note that such consultants will bring their own biases. At the least, they will have an interest in ensuring the evaluation meets the requirements of the donor, or whoever is paying for it.

It is increasingly recognised that evaluation can play a much more positive role in the development process when it is seen as a participatory process involving all the stakeholders, rather than an external examination. In order for communities and groups of people to engage in long term sustainable development, they must be included throughout the cycle of action-reflection-action. Rather than only providing management information, evaluation should move to a process of informing and assisting the primary stakeholders in the development process and become an instrument for mutual accountability. Like monitoring, evaluation should be a participatory process involving a wide range of stakeholders at every stage, from establishing the terms of reference to reviewing the recommendations.

In a participatory evaluation, the role of the evaluator (or evaluation team) is focused on facilitation rather than judgement. A monitoring and evaluation system which has monitoring at its core should be able to provide required data at the time of evaluation. With effective monitoring in place, the focus of evaluation can become the analysis and review of existing data sources rather than the desperate rush to gather new information – to recreate the project's history over the past five years, for example. The evaluation process can provide an opportunity for dialogue between stakeholders as they put forward their different views and experience of the project.

The report from such an evaluation is a result of negotiation between the different stakeholders, rather than simply the views of the evaluators. The evaluation may still present judgements about the project but, unlike a conventional evaluation, they are arising primarily from those involved in the project. It follows that as a participatory process involving mutual accountability the evaluation process should be transparent – the reports and recommendations should be disseminated to all major stakeholders, in particular the proposed beneficiaries of the intervention.

The Evaluation Terms of Reference

Unlike monitoring, evaluation usually involves people who are not engaged in the normal day to day running of the project. Although evaluation should be seen as a process, it is an exercise which takes place over a set time and involves people working outside their normal roles. It is therefore very important that everybody knows what the evaluation is looking at and what their particular role is to be in it. The document which describes these and other parameters for an evaluation is known as the *terms of reference*. It can be seen as the equivalent of a job description for those taking part in the evaluation. Box 3 shows an outline terms of reference from one donor NGO that is used for commissioning evaluations from external consultants. Terms of reference should be prepared not only for external consultants, but also other members of staff who are breaking from their normal duties to take part in the evaluation. It may take a considerable length of time to negotiate the terms reference and there must be allowances for this when planning an evaluation.

The terms of reference is an important document as it makes clear the purpose and scope of the evaluation, what is expected from those taking part and how their work will be assessed. This last point is crucial as whoever is commissioning the evaluation must be able to ensure that the work is carried out to an appropriate standard. If no assessment of the evaluation is put in place, a poor evaluation based on weak evidence may bring forward recommendations that are not appropriate for the project and cause more harm than good.

If an evaluation is to be participatory, then this approach should start with the preparation of the terms of reference. These should represent the output of a participatory process, where different primary stakeholders have been consulted about their priorities for evaluation. This may simply be a set of brief meetings or workshops with different groups to establish the purpose and scope of the evaluation. Appropriate questions for such meetings might include:

- What aspects of the project are going well?

- What are the areas where the project is running into difficulty?

- Are there particular aspect of the project which should change?

These should be brought together into a draft terms of reference which should be circulated to the various stakeholders for their comment. It is important to strike a balance between the effort which goes into agreeing the terms of reference and the actual effort required for the evaluation itself. In practice, given the difficulties of communications and time constraints, the final terms of reference are likely to be drawn up at the head office. However, if they reflect the views of the primary stakeholders, it will make the whole process of evaluation much easier. Wherever the final terms of reference are prepared they should be communicated to the field staff and other primary stakeholders as soon as possible – certainly before the evaluation begins.

Unfortunately, it is still common for evaluation teams to be put together and sent on field visits with a clear terms of reference, but on arrival they find that nobody in the field has seen these terms of reference. This immediately creates a distance between the evaluation team and local stakeholders, who may know very little about why these visitors have come and what they want. Rather than being able to facilitate a process of reflection and analysis which has already started, the evaluators are then faced with the choice of trying to start the process from scratch or carrying on using the externally imposed terms of reference. The former approach will require the renegotiation of the terms of reference in the field. This may well be impossible in the time available and it may be difficult for them to vary greatly from the initial terms of reference which they are contracted to fulfil.

Box 3: *Outline for terms of reference for project evaluation* (adapted from Tearfund)

Basic information
- Project title
- Background to project
- Summary findings of previous reports, evaluations
- Current activities

Purpose and scope of the evaluation
- The goal of the evaluation.
- Specific objectives of the evaluation – what questions should it answer, e.g.
    Is delivery of project outputs leading to achievements of objectives?
    Is achievement of project objectives helping to achieve project purpose?
    What lessons can be learned from the project?
    How effective are monitoring systems?
    To what levels are project users participating in all stages of the project – planning, implementation, management?
    Are project objectives being achieved at a reasonable financial cost?
    Is the project sustainable?

Methodology
- Who should define the methodology – the organisation commissioning the evaluation, the evaluation team leader, the project stakeholders?
- What methodology – interviews, surveys, research, group discussions etc.? To what extent is the evaluation expected to be participatory? How will the views of those who might be marginalised be included? Where possible be specific, for instance naming the individuals and groups to be interviewed, detailing how a questionnaire will be written and tested, and used.

Scheduling
- Dates for:
    - briefing and de-briefing
    - travel
    - submission of final report and any presentation
- Itinerary for the planned visit, who, when and where

Management of visit
- The person who is responsible for commissioning and approving the work – the 'client'
- The person to whom the consultant should refer to resolve issues as they arise
- The person responsible for practical arrangements such as travel, hotels etc.

Expected output
- How direct feedback should be given to the partner
- Format of final report
- Scope of recommendations – to whom should the report be making recommendations, e.g. project staff, donor, other stakeholders. For each group include:
    a) Recommendations on issues to be addressed now; and
    b) Recommendations on what should be done next time (lessons learnt for the future)

Required inputs
- People to be involved (partners, community leaders, government officials) and their roles
- Other consultancy team members (where relevant)

Review of the evaluation
- Who will provide feedback on how the evaluation process went, and when?
- Who will review and comment on the report?

Putting Together an Evaluation Team

Once a draft terms of reference is in place, so that the purpose, scope and evaluation approach have been agreed, it is possible to start putting together the evaluation team. The size and composition of the evaluation team will depend on the size of the project, the scope of the evaluation, the time and budget available. The larger the team, the longer time and more effort will be required in setting up the evaluation.

For many evaluations, it is helpful if it is led by somebody who is not a stakeholder in the project (or whatever is to be evaluated – programme, strategy, relationship). Outsiders may be able to:

- Bring insights from experience beyond that available within the project – from other regions or countries, various NGOs, and possibly different sectors.

- Question practices which may be taken for granted by insiders – any project may establish patterns of behaviour or relationships which people get used to and come to accept without question.

- Review the monitoring data with a fresh eye – a project's stakeholders are likely to be too familiar with the monitoring data to be able to gain an overview of it.

- Raise concerns which might be seen as too sensitive or political for insiders who may have a particular interest in the issue – an evaluation team can meet with people in confidence and provide a safe forum for people to air views which they may feel unable to do with project staff or senior management.

However, if an evaluation team only consists of outsiders, it is likely to suffer from some disadvantages:

- Limited knowledge of the project area and the local social, economic and political context that may have a very significant effect on the project's outcome – for example, inheritance practices, or ethnic relations.

- Limited understanding of the project's roots and history – many aspects of a social development project may have been shaped by past experience and events, only some of which is documented in the project's records.

- No personal contacts with stakeholders – an outsider may be a complete stranger who has never met the people concerned with the project.

An evaluation team will pick up some understanding of the local context, the project history and the people during the evaluation but it may make their job more difficult. To get round these problems, it is often helpful to use a team which includes one or more insiders who are already familiar with the project.

It is important to consider the mix of qualities, skills and experience which are required by the people doing the evaluation. These will vary according to the terms of reference. For example, an evaluation which is focusing on the efficiency of a labour based road build-ing project will require one of the team members to have technical expertise in civil engi-neering to assess whether the complete road is of an appropriate quality – could a technically better result have been achieved by using machinery? It will also require a person with expertise in sociology or household economics to assess the cost to participants who put their time into building the road – could they have more profitably spent their time on other business? In general, it has been found that a multidisciplinary team is more likely to obtain a wide range of views than a team composed of people coming from the same disci-pline.

Apart from the basic training of the people, it is also important to consider their back-ground and experience. Are they familiar with the project area? Do they have experience of evaluations of the type planned? Do they speak the appropriate languages? As far as possi-ble the team should include a balance of women and men.

Particular attention needs to be paid to the selection of the team leader. However participatory the evaluation, it will be necessary to have one person who is responsible to drive it forward and guide it through the various difficulties which will come up on the way. In particular the team leader is usually responsible for the final production of the evaluation report. For a participatory evaluation it is therefore important to select a team leader who is used to working as a facilitator rather than an 'expert'.

It may be a great challenge for many NGOs to identify appropriate external candidates to take part in an evaluation. Often they will draw on consultants or others who are known to them already. Other sources include:

- Staff of other NGOs – especially those involved in similar projects in the same area. They are likely to bring a good local knowledge and understanding of the work. Involving them in the evaluation will help to disseminate lessons from the project within the area and help co-operation between NGOs. This type of peer evaluation will only be possible where there is a good open relationship between NGOs rather than competition.

- University researchers – often they may undertake some consultancy in addition to their research and teaching work. They may be able to provide a high level of knowledge and good quality analysis. It is important to ensure that they have some grounding in the practical application of theory and are able to relate directly to the primary stakeholders.

Whichever candidates are approached, it will be necessary to negotiate about terms and conditions for the evaluation. They will need to be contacted well in advance of the evalua-tion to ensure that they have sufficient time to prepare. Often the composition of the final team may be as much determined by practical issues, such as costs (fees and travel) and

Box 4: *Checklist for commissioning and managing an evaluation*
(adapted from Tearfund 2000)

PRE-EVALUATION
- Plan at the beginning of the project when there should be an evaluation
- Allow for the cost of evaluation in the budget – include fees, travel, accommodation etc.
- Draw up table listing primary and secondary stakeholders, their interests and which interests are priorities
- Discuss timing, type and scope of evaluation with other stakeholders well in advance of the evaluation
- List possible threats to the evaluation process and ways of overcoming them

Draw up terms of reference
- Draw up a table with the question areas to be covered, and justification as to why each is important
- Decide who should draw up the proposed evaluation methodology (all stakeholders, organisation commissioning evaluation, the evaluation team leader, etc.)
- Send draft to all stakeholders to comment, giving date for comments to be received
- Redraft ToR taking into account views of all stakeholders and send final ToR to all stakeholders

Identify and select potential team members
- Draw up list of essential and desirable qualities in team members in discussion with stakeholders
- Identify and contact possible team members to assess their suitability, fee rates and availability for the assignment
- Ensure suggested team includes both men and women
- Draw up short job description for team leader and team members
- Check with the team leader of the evaluation that the ToR can be completed, discuss methodology and ensure that the time for writing the report is adequate
- Draw up contracts for consultants

Administration
- Finalise the budget for the evaluation
- Draw up itinerary for the evaluation process
- Confirm dates of travel and ensure practical arrangements for travel are made – e.g. check flights are available, visas obtained, accommodation is booked
- Send copies of background documents to team members (paper or email)
- Check that where possible meetings are arranged in advance, e.g. with local officials
- Draw up a list of contact numbers and addresses for the team members whilst on the visit

Send to team members prior to briefing
- Background information on organisation and project and extract from planning and strategy documents
- List of contact numbers and addresses

Briefing of team members
- Confirm that the team leader will be responsible for the completed report
- Ask the team members to clarify what they think is expected by the evaluation
- Discuss how project users and other stakeholders will participate in the evaluation
- Discuss exactly what outputs will be provided (what type of presentations, workshops, report etc.)

timing, as by the ideal mix of skills and experience.

Each person's role in the evaluation team must be made clear in their contract, for external members, or a specific section of the terms of reference, for internal people. This should detail what they are expected to do, how long it will take and the conditions of payment. It is important that each person's responsibilities outside the main period of the evaluation are made clear – are they expected to attend debriefing meetings, what is their role in preparation of the report? Very often the evaluation team leader may be made responsible for submission of the evaluation report but he or she may need other team members to write particular sections or give feedback on drafts. It is easier if these things are spelt out in advance as far as possible.

Managing Evaluations

Preparation
Most organisations never leave enough time to prepare for an evaluation, even for long running social development projects. The length of time required to go through the first phases of setting up the evaluation – negotiating the terms of reference, identifying team members – will usually be much more than that taken by the actual evaluation itself. A participatory evaluation is likely to need more time to ensure that a wide range of stake-holders is consulted. Up to a year may be required to prepare a big evaluation involving a large team. Box 4 shows a checklist of points for those managing evaluations to bear in mind in preparing for an evaluation.

During the Evaluation
How the actual evaluation exercise should be managed will depend greatly on the scope of the evaluation and the methods used. More detail about the process of data collection is given in Part 2, but there are also some practical issues which are important to consider:

- How many project sites can be visited? It may be necessary to select a sample of project sites rather than visit them all. As soon as it known that this may be the case, the project participants in each site should be advised that not all of them will be included. Once the list of actual field visits has been finalised this should be passed on to all areas. As far as possible, the criteria for selection of sites should be made clear. This is to avoid the disappointment which participants may feel at not taking part in the actual evaluation, especially if they have participated in the preparation.

- If the team is large it may be possible to maximise their coverage of field sites in the time available by splitting the team and arranging simultaneous visits to different sites.

- Be careful not to overwhelm field staff and other stakeholders – a field office with two staff may find it difficult to host an evaluation team of four people as they struggle to arrange accommodation, transport and office space. The logistics of dealing with the visit may distract attention from the purpose of the visit.

- Ensure that sufficient time is included for analysis and reflection during the evaluation. It is tempting to assume that the evaluation team should be out in the field for most of the time. However, there must be periods where they can meet together as a team to reflect on their progress and findings so far.

- The evaluation team should aim as far as possible to present their preliminary findings and conclusions in each of the field sites they visit. The format will depend on the methods being used. Where participatory methods with a high level of community analysis is involved the findings will be produced by all the participants. If more individual interviews or survey methods are used, it may be more appropriate to call together a stakeholder meeting before leaving the area.

- At the end of the evaluation fieldwork, the evaluation team should present their findings, conclusions and recommendations to the primary stakeholders. This is important to ensure that the stakeholders have a chance to clarify any points or correct any misunderstandings. It will help the evaluation team get a sense of the validity of their findings. After such a debriefing which outlines the recommendations, the final evaluation report should not contain any major surprises.

After the Evaluation

Box 5 gives a checklist of some of the management issues to be addressed after an evaluation. One of the major advantages of participatory evaluation over a more conventional approach is that much of the value of the exercise is provided through the actual evaluation process – the interviews, meetings, workshops which take place – as most of the analysis is undertaken by the stakeholders and they own the results. These are major outputs of an evaluation. The evaluation report may not contain anything new but it is still very important:

- It is the written record of the evaluation and will enable the learning from the exercise to be passed on within the project and organisation as staff and other stakeholders change;

- The report may be the main form of communicating the results of the evaluation to more distant stakeholders such as donors or government departments. They may have a very limited appreciation of the process underlying the evaluation but they may use the report to make judgements about the project – in particular to make funding decisions;

- The document will enable the lessons from the project to be disseminated more widely and possibly feed into wider practice.

It is therefore very important that the management of the evaluation does not finish abruptly once the evaluation team departs. There needs to be some procedure in place for

Box 5: *Checklist for post-evaluation management (adapted from Tearfund)*

POST-EVALUATION

Managing the report

- Receive and check the quality of the report
- Circulate report to other stakeholders and ask for comments by certain date
- Meet evaluation team members and discuss draft recommendations from the report
- Discuss any areas of the report you disagree with, or don't understand
- Agree on revisions to the report and check that these are made in the final report

Implement/reject recommendations

- Review the recommendations with stakeholders and agree which should be accepted or rejected with reasons
- Check what extra resources will be needed in order to implement changes
- Three months after the evaluation, check that the recommendations have been followed up

Review evaluation process

- Ask for feedback on the process of evaluation from stakeholders and the evaluation team
- Provide feedback to team members on basis of the feedback from stakeholders and reading of report
- Provide written comment on report to team leader within two weeks of receipt of report

---

dealing with the production of the report and following up its recommendations. The actual report outputs should have been specified in the terms of reference.

The organisation commissioning the evaluation should make sure that it has assigned somebody to be responsible for receiving the report and checking that it meets the specifications required. The draft of the report should be circulated to stakeholders for comments. Their comments must be passed back to the evaluation team so they can make any necessary changes to the report.

It is very unlikely that any evaluation report will meet with the approval of everybody. The final report will be the product of negotiation. If the evaluation contains findings which are uncomfortable for powerful stakeholders, such as the donor or the NGO running the project, it is important that the evaluation team is not put under pressure to remove them – if they are valid conclusions.

How widely the report should be circulated in its draft form may need careful consideration. It will be impractical to ask for feedback on the report from all of those who contributed to the evaluation. If there are contentious findings, it is helpful if they are not widely publicised until the primary stakeholders have agreed that they are valid or they have had an opportunity to respond. Good practice for participatory evaluations would suggest that the circulation should be as wide as possible and certainly include field staff and some of the project participants.

Once the evaluation report has been accepted (and it is usual not to make a final payment to the evaluation team leader until it has been), the stakeholders have to deal with the recommendations that have been made. This is a critical stage of the evaluation process which is often neglected. Any organisation undertaking an evaluation needs to have in place a system for reviewing and responding to its recommendations to ensure that the learning is incorporated into practice. Recommendations should either be accepted and acted upon, or rejected. Ideally there should be some formal mechanism in place for ensuring that recommendations are followed up in practice and not left as good intentions. For an NGO it may be appropriate to have evaluation reports reviewed by the board overseeing the work of the NGO and the board holding the NGO's management to account for responding to the recommendations.

Finally, it is very useful for an NGO to undertake some review of the evaluation process itself. Did the evaluation achieve its purpose as stated in the terms of reference? What lessons can be learned from the way the evaluation was carried out? How can the process be improved for the future? These and other issues of incorporating learning from the monitoring and evaluation system are discussed in more detail in Chapter 8.

PART 2
Managing Information

Information is the essential fuel required to drive forward any monitoring and evaluation system. In this second part of the guide, we turn to look more closely at how we can ensure that we have the right information, in the right quantities, at the place to make the system work. Chapter 4 lays out some basic principles for dealing with information and then Chapters 5–8 by turn look at the processes of selecting data, collecting data, analysing it and putting it to use.

Chapter 4 starts by highlighting the importance of thinking about why you are collecting the information and the potential users of it, prior to any data collection. It then gives some general principles for managing data. These include the principle of optimal ignorance, ensuring data is reliable, valid and credible, and triangulation.

Chapter 5 moves on to consider how to decide what information should be collected within the monitoring and evaluation system. It defines indicators and their characteristics and outlines a participatory process for identifying appropriate indicators.

In Chapter 6 the focus shifts to gathering the information and outlines various data collection methods. It describes some of the factors which will influence the choice of tools used for collecting data. It introduces the techniques of sampling and gives some broad guidelines for how to approach people when collecting data. In the rest of the chapter some qualitative and quantitative tools are introduced, including various forms of interviews, surveys and participatory methods.

Chapter 7 turns to look at the process of analysis of the data collected for monitoring and evaluation. Analysis involves five steps – reviewing data, summarising data, interrogating data, learning from the data and taking action. The first three of these are the focus of this chapter. It introduces qualitative and quantitative data analysis, and discusses how the findings can be consolidated into an overall picture of the project's progress from which lessons can be drawn. It concludes with some suggestions for the presentation of the findings.

The final chapter of this part returns to the four reasons for monitoring and evaluation laid out in the Introduction: accountability, improving performance, learning, and communication. For each of these, it briefly suggests how the data collected in the monitoring and evaluation system can be put to good use to bring about change.

CHAPTER 4

General Principles and Guidelines for Dealing with Data

The Context of Information Management

Before trying to collect any information or do anything with it, it is important to consider two basic points which will provide the context for obtaining information: why is the information required and who will be using the information? Reflecting on these points will help in making decisions about what data to collect and how to collect it.

Why is the Information Needed?

The first stage in managing any data is to decide why you want it in the first place. This is a major challenge in any monitoring and evaluation system, as it is easy to set up an elaborate system, which will gather masses of data but only a small portion of it will be necessary (see Box 6). The reason for collecting data must be kept in mind throughout the other steps for managing information.

The purpose behind information gathering for monitoring and evaluation is to answer a set of questions. The range and nature of the questions will vary with the organisation, the stakeholders and the project or programme.

Box 6: *The dilemma of choosing data for evaluating micro-finance*

The case of micro-finance is interesting. There is an ongoing debate about the best way of assessing the impact of projects which support the establishment of micro-finance institutions (MFIs). A vital aspect of such projects is that the MFI should be sustainable and give loans at interest rates which cover their costs. If the MFI wants to look into the impact of loans at the household level, it may be necessary to ask questions such as, how is the loan used? how does it change household income? who controls the loan in the household?

Answering these questions would require considerable extra work as it is likely to involve interviewing a wide range of clients or conduct expensive surveys. Many involved in micro-finance argue that this is not necessary. The number of people who return for repeat loans will show if there is a positive impact – if people did not find loans beneficial they would only take one once!

It may be helpful to write down some of the questions you are hoping to answer through the monitoring and evaluation system. These may be general questions such as:

- What project outputs have been delivered?
- Is the project achieving its objectives?
- What proportion of the budget has been spent?
- Is the project sustainable?

Or specific questions related to the particular project under consideration:

- How are people using the new services provided by the project?
- What has been the average change in beneficiaries' household income?
- How has the new water source affected gender relations in the community?

It is likely that there will be too many questions to answer and it will be necessary to prioritise the most critical areas for which information is required.

When you start working out how to answer these questions, it may become clear that there is no easy way to answer some of them. In some cases, there may be no reliable way to gather the information, and in others, the methods required would be too time consuming and expensive for the project. Such questions will have to be dropped and the ambitions of the monitoring and evaluation system will have to be pulled back. This will not be a problem as long as it is possible to answer some questions about the efficiency, effect and impact of the project. However, if it proves impossible to find any questions that can be answered concerning the project's impact, this must call into doubt the project design.

Who is the information for?

Ideally, monitoring and evaluation information is used by a wide range of people including project management, project users, donors and other stakeholders. Their requirements for information must be considered when planning the monitoring and evaluation system. The information must be:

- *Comprehensible* – different stakeholders will be able to understand different types of information. Donors may have a limited knowledge of the situation in the field and will require more description of the context than project participants. Project participants may not be familiar with technical terms.

- *Manageable* – the stakeholders might be perfectly able to understand the monitoring and evaluation information, but they may have very limited time available to look at it. It is important to have realistic expectations of the time and effort you can expect stakeholders to dedicate to the monitoring and evaluation process.

Having worked out why you want to gather data and intended audience (or consumers) the following steps will need to be considered:

- **Data selection** – what information will you need to gather? The main focus here is on establishing the indicators required to answer the questions.

- **Data collection** – how will the data be gathered? There are many different techniques of data collection which are appropriate in different circumstances.

- **Data analysis** – how will the data be analysed? Collecting data will achieve little unless it is analysed in order to bring answers to the questions.

- **Data use** – how will the data be used? Analysing the data and producing reports will not have any value if the information is not used to change things.

These steps are covered in detail in the following chapters in this section. There must be a balance between the effort put into data selection, collection, analysis and use. Spending a lot of time deciding what data is required and how it should be collected will not be of any use, if the actual data collection exercise is not given adequate resources. Gathering all the data and then having no time or expertise to analyse it, will mean that the information sits at the bottom of a drawer. Performing a detailed analysis of the raw data and producing clear and comprehensive reports will achieve little, if nobody will read them or make changes in the light of the findings.

For the information to be useful it will need to have the following qualities:

- **Content** – the information must have some substantive content which says something beyond the self-evident. It must be relevant to the question under consideration and be reliable and credible. For example, information from an unreliable survey may only serve to confuse rather than given any clear picture of what is happening.

- **Accessibility** – the information must be presented in a format that can be understood by others and stored in a way so that others can retrieve it. For example, a very high quality survey which uses coded responses to a questionnaire may be of very limited use if the coding system is not stored with the responses. Reports presented using technical jargon which is not understood by most stakeholders will not be useful. If the information is not stored properly but remains in the heads of those who collected it, it will disappear when those people leave the organisation or move on from the project.

To make this point more strongly Britton distinguishes between information, and knowledge and wisdom on the basis of how the information is processed and combined with experience[1]:

- **'Information** – This is the simple fragmented raw material of facts, opinions and ideas of which knowledge is made.

---

[1] Britton 1998: 4.

- **Knowledge** – Systematically organised information which, by the processes of analysis, comparison, testing and generalising can be used to answer complex questions.

- **Wisdom** – This involves uniting the facts and insights of knowledge with the fruits of experience in a way which can usefully guide action (for example, through the development of procedures, policies, and particular approaches to work).

Information only has *value* when it is converted into knowledge. Knowledge becomes *precious* when it is combined with experience to produce wisdom which can be used to guide action. However, even wisdom has limitations if it is locked in the minds of individuals and not shared with others.'

Some General Principles on Handling Data

When designing the monitoring and evaluation system for social development projects, it is useful to bear in mind the general principles outlined here. These principles will run through the following chapters on data selection, collection, analysis and use.

Optimal Ignorance or Good Enough Data

The task of data collection can become overwhelming, if too much is expected. The monitoring and evaluation system should focus on finding out what we need to know, not everything we might like to know. In the example from micro-finance given above, the questions about household interactions might be very interesting but if they are not required for monitoring and evaluation they should not be included in the system.

The monitoring and evaluation system is aiming only to be good enough. It will not answer all the interesting questions about the project. An effective and efficient system will aim for 'optimal ignorance' (Chambers 1983). In practice, there are no universal rules for achieving the balance between being overwhelmed and not having sufficient information with which to make a judgement. It is a question of working out the minimum amount of information required which will produce sufficient evidence for the purposes of monitoring and evaluation.

Keep Things as Simple as Possible

Dealing with data should not be the preserve of specialists and experts to the exclusion of others, especially in a participatory monitoring and evaluation system. Although some types of data analysis may require specialist knowledge, many do not. Where there are alternatives it is usually better to choose the simplest route to answering the questions of concern. For example, if the cost effectiveness of an investment in a development activity is being assessed, it is possible to use technical financial calculations such as net present value and internal rates of return. However, the equivalent information may be presented using simple comparisons of income and expenditure. The latter analysis may not be so technically advanced but it may be equally valid.[2]

Plan for the Whole Process of Data Handling

As far as possible all the stages of managing information should be considered before any data is collected. Otherwise it is too easy to put a lot of effort into gathering and analysing data and then find that there is no clear way to use it. All stakeholders should be involved in this process to ensure that they agree not only on the indicators but also the methods being used to collect data. Otherwise it may be difficult to agree on the findings produced through monitoring or evaluation and this will make it more difficult to agree on response to them.

For example, the donor may be expecting monitoring to be based on counting the number of people using the project services, whereas the project participants may be more interested in narrative testimonies. If monitoring focuses on the former, it may show that the number of users is increasing and the donor may believe that the project is succeeding. However, if the experience of the users is often negative, they may press for changes, which the donor does not think are necessary. Such problems can be avoided by thinking through the whole process of managing data from the outset.

Reliable, Valid and Credible Information

As far as possible, information used in the monitoring and evaluation system should be reliable, valid and credible.

- **Reliable** – data is reliable when you can be confident that you will get very similar results if you repeated the data collection exercise within the same time period, using the same methods.

  As far as possible, the information should not be dependent on the person who is collecting it. You must be confident that if two different people had carried out the same exercise, each would have found largely the same findings. This is difficult to check on. In any interview, the way that the question is phrased and even the tone of voice used, may change the response. Likewise, some observers will notice some things more than others. For example, a woman who is observing a meeting dominated by men, may make many more observations about gender relations evident in the interaction, than a man in the same position.

- **Valid** – data is valid when it accurately measures (or describes) what it set out to measure (or describe). Monitoring may *reliably* show that the project participants are finding the service provided by the project very useful. However, these findings may not be *valid*, if they are the result of asking project participants leading questions such as, 'Are you happy with the project's services?' (see Chapter 6).

  Threats to validity include failing to gather data from a representative group of stakeholders, claiming general results from limited sources of evidence,

---

[2] If not more so, as it avoids the hidden assumptions buried in the interest rates used in NPV and IRR.

misunderstanding between those collecting data and the participants. For example, an evaluation will not get an accurate picture of the project's activities by only considering the groups which are continuing. There may be many more that have stopped working for reasons which need to be investigated.

- **Credible** – data is credible when it is believable and is compatible with a 'common sense' view of the world. The results of monitoring and evaluation should fit with realistic expectations of what a project might achieve. If an evaluation of an income generating project claims to show that average household incomes have doubled within one year as a result of the project, this would be a remarkable result and might not be credible. The credibility of data can be increased by providing further details, which show why the project is generating such significant or unexpected results.

  Checking results of monitoring and evaluation for credibility will help to pick up errors which may have occurred in the analysis. It is important to note because data is not credible does not mean that it is necessarily inaccurate or false. Sometimes, a project will act as a catalyst to produce very significant results, out of all proportion to the project inputs.

In summary, problems with the validity of data are usually the result of the monitoring and evaluation system being poorly designed. Data will be unreliable if data is collected carelessly. Credibility will become a problem when the system does not have sufficient checks to make sure that the results make sense.

Triangulation

Triangulation is a very useful technique for improving the quality of information used in the monitoring and evaluation system. When you are trying to accurately locate a place on the ground, if you have a bearing to it from three separate points you will be able to pinpoint exactly where it is. Although this precise technique of triangulation will not apply in social settings where there may not be objective facts to find out, a similar principle is used to

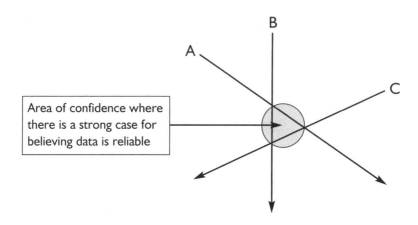

Area of confidence where there is a strong case for believing data is reliable

achieve reliability in data collection. If the findings from three different sources are consistent, this suggests that the data is reliable and portrays a good picture of the situation. This cross checking through triangulation should be built into the monitoring and evaluation system to ensure that it builds up an accurate picture of the project. There are a number of ways of achieving the three different perspectives required for triangulation (see Roche 1999: 86):

- **Using different sources of information** – this is the most common form of triangulation where information is cross checked with different people. This may involve talking to different people in a community, comparing the situation of different communities, or looking at the perspective of different stakeholders.

- **Using different methods of data collection** – mixing qualitative and quantitative techniques, or formal and less formal participatory methods generates different types of data which should be consistent. These different methods are outlined in the following chapter.

- **Using different people to collect data** – at times the findings can be affected by the individual collecting information, especially when using qualitative methods which rely heavily on interviews or other personal interactions. If different people carrying out a set of interviews come up with similar findings this builds confidence in their reliability.

Triangulation of information in social development projects will not necessarily be a by smooth process and contradictions are likely to occur. These may be a result of faulty data collection or reflect the bias of different stakeholders. In some cases these may be easily explained but in others they will highlight areas which need further investigation.

Units of Analysis

Before collecting and analysing data, it is necessary to decide at what level information should be gathered. Should the monitoring system look at the outputs delivered for each individual, household, a community group, or the whole community? At what level should an evaluation explore the impact of the project? For a capacity building project, it may be more appropriate to look at the changes occurring in community based organisations. For a social development project aiming to improve household incomes, the household may be a more suitable level. For projects which are concerned with organisational development within an NGO, the changes within the NGO should be monitored and evaluated.

The decisions about the appropriate units of analysis can only be made after consideration of the particular aims and objectives of the project, and the context in which it is operating. It should also be noted that there are practical advantages and disadvantages to different units of analysis, which should be borne in mind. Some of these are summarised in Table 5. Usually information will be gathered at more one than one level and this will contribute to the triangulation of the results.

Table 5: *Advantages and disadvantages of different levels of analysis*
(Adapted from Roche 1999: 53)

Unit of analysis	Advantages	Disadvantages
Individual	Easily defined and identified. Gender relations and relations within households can be explored. Can allow personal and intimate issues to emerge.	Difficult to speak to representative sample, including the most marginalised people. May involve large numbers of people and be expensive. Difficult to gain wider picture of household or community level.
Household	Permits appreciation of income, asset, consumption and labour pooling. Permits appreciation of link between individual, household and group/community. Permits understanding of links between household life-cycle and well-being.	Exact membership is sometimes difficult to assess. Often results in only talking to household head which may result in bias – especially gender bias. Difficult to take account of relationships within household.
Community based organisation	Involves activists who are likely to be willing participants in monitoring and evaluation. Permits understanding of collective action. Permits understanding of changes brought about by capacity-building.	Group dynamics are often difficult to understand. Difficult to make comparisons between organisations. Likely to be biased to view of activists – difficult to relate experience of CBO whole members to that of community.
Community or village	Permits understanding of differences within the community and faction and clan relations. Can act as sampling frame for household/individual assessments.	Difficult to identify sources of information for whole community. Exact boundary is sometimes difficult to assess. Community dynamics are often difficult to understand. Difficult to compare communities.
Local NGO	Permits understanding of changes brought about by capacity building. Allows assessment of performance (especially in terms of effectiveness and efficiency). Allows exploration of links between change at the community, group, and the individual level.	NGO dynamics are difficult to understand. Difficult to compare various local NGOs.

CHAPTER 5

Data Selection

This chapter is concerned with the process of identifying the information that needs to be collected for monitoring or evaluating a social development project. As noted in the previous chapter, the information required will vary depending on the broad questions that it is expected to address, and who is expected to use it. We now move on to the next stage, to consider in more detail how to identify exactly what data we need to gather.

The major challenge is to find appropriate indicators for monitoring and evaluating the project. Recall from Chapter 1, that an indicator is simply an observable change or event which provides evidence that something has happened as a result of the project intervention. The choice of indicators will determine the information which is required.

Key Questions

A social development project will start with a view to addressing a particular problem or situation which needs to change. As a first step towards identifying indicators, it is helpful to draw up a list of key questions whose answers will give an idea of the progress that has been made in relation to delivering outputs, achieving the objectives, and contributing to the goal.

These questions may be refined from the list of broader questions drawn up at the beginning of Chapter 4 to help think through the purpose of data collection. Key questions should be posed at the level of effort, effect and change (see Chapter 1):

Effort – what interventions have been started to address the situation?

Effect – how have these interventions been used and received by the target population?

Change – what evidence is there that the situation has changed?

For example, one of the objectives of a programme for capacity building for community based organisations and NGOs is:

To strengthen the organisational capacity and independence of existing and new community based organisations and NGOs.

In a workshop with stakeholders, the following key questions were put forward to assess progress in achieving this objective:

- Are the services provided by NGOs appropriate, high quality and demand led?

- What organisational capacities and skills have been strengthened?

With these questions in mind, the workshop participants were then able to suggest appropriate indicators for the programme; gathering data on changes in these indicators will provide the answers to the key questions.

Key question	Indicators
Are the services provided by NGOs appropriate, high quality and demand led?	No. of appeals and degree of satisfaction No. of issues solved Acknowledgement by clients Image of the organisation
What organisational capacities and skills have been strengthened?	Changes in organisational structure Changes to system of work Changes in management practices Levels of transparency and accountability

Definition of Indicators

Before going further into the selection of indicators, we must define them more carefully. In this guide we take the following definition of an indicator:

> In the context of social development projects, an indicator is an observable change or event, which provides evidence that something has happened – whether an output delivered, immediate effect occurred or long term change observed.

An indicator does not provide proof so much as a reliable sign that the event or process being claimed has actually happened (or is happening). The evidence from a number of indicators will provide the convincing case for the claims being made.

It may be possible to find indicators which directly relate to the claim being made. For example, if an output of the project is that ten new businesses will be established by project participants, the number of new businesses actually established will be a direct indicator of progress.

In many cases, it may not be so simple to show progress, especially when it comes to showing progress toward project objectives or goals. For example, if the objective is to improve the capacity of the community development committee, there is no simple direct indicator. The indicators used may be measures such as an increase in the attendance at meetings and the start of new activities initiated by the committee. There is a reasonable case for arguing that these indicators are related to an increase in capacity. Such indicators are known as *proxy* indicators.

Proxy indicators may also be required when the direct information is not accessible for some reason. For example, if an education project aims to reduce the prevalence of teenage sexual activity with the goal of reducing the prevalence of HIV/AIDS, it will be impossible accurately to find out the number of sexually active teenagers. Instead progress may be measured through proxy indicators, such as the number of teenage pregnancies and the number of reported cases of sexually transmitted diseases among teenagers.

Characteristics of Indicators

There are two broad types of indicators, quantitative and qualitative. Both forms of indicator will contribute to the picture of the situation and will be required in the monitoring and evaluation of social development. Both quantitative and qualitative indicators will be needed.

Quantitative indicators are those which are expressed as numbers. For example:

- Units – the number of staff that have been trained

- Prices – the amount of money that was spent on building

- Proportions – the proportion of the community that has access to the service (usually expressed as a percentage)

- Rates of change – the percentage change in average household income over the reporting period

- Scoring and ranking – the score out of five given by the project participants to rate the quality of the service they receive

Qualitative indicators are those which are expressed through narrative description. For example:

- Satisfaction – how participants describe their levels of satisfaction with the project's activities

- Standards – the extent to which training is recognised by the appropriate authorities

- Practices and behaviour – the way practice has changed since the completion of hygiene education

- Institutional change – the new measures introduced to improve the NGO's accountability to project users

Both qualitative and quantitative indicators have different strengths and weaknesses. Some of these are summarised below.

Qualitative data	
Strengths	**Weaknesses**
Lends itself to being collected and analysed in a participatory manner Focuses on ordinary events in natural settings so draws a more detailed picture of events, processes Since the information has been collected close to a specific situation it is grounded in people's real life experiences Can describe processes over time and provide explanations for changes Can record the meaning people place on events, processes and structures of their lives Useful for validating, explaining or reinterpreting quantitative data gathered from the same setting	Difficult to record in a consistent way Difficult to analyse and make comparisons between situations May not be able to paint an overall picture of what is happening

Quantitative data	
Strengths	**Weaknesses**
Easy to record data Can use standard forms of analysis (statistics) Data can be easily compared between different sources Can give a broad overview of the situation Can raise further questions for further investigation	Data is not set in any context so it is difficult to identify and correct any mistakes when they occur Cannot answer questions about why things occur Difficult to collect and analyse in a participatory manner

It often appears as if these two categories are completely separate, so that information is either quantitative or qualitative. However, there is some overlap as qualitative data can often be represented quantitatively in some way. For example, if the data is collected about participants' views of the project impact, it might be possible to classify their responses as positive (+1), negative (-1) and neutral (0). This can then be seen as a quantitative scoring indicator and analysed using quantitative methods (see Chapter 7). Likewise, it would be possible to start with a list of behaviour changes, which it is hoped will be observed during the project. This list could be compared with the observed changes in behaviour and the proportion of expected changes recorded.

In general, converting qualitative data into a quantitative form will simplify the data for analysis – but information will be lost in the process. For example, if the participants' views are classified as simply positive, negative or neutral, any information about the reasons they gave for their responses will not be recorded. Qualitative data can be described as rich data like rich food – more difficult to obtain and harder to digest, but worth the effort.

In order to be useful within a monitoring and evaluation system, both quantitative and qualitative indicators should have the following characteristics. They should be:

- **Specific** – indicators should be specifically related to areas in which the project is expected to make some difference, avoiding measures that are largely subject to external influences. For example, if a project is aiming to strengthen a cooperative's membership, indicators of achievement may include the level of members' participation in general meetings.

- **Unambiguous** – indicators must be clearly defined so that their measurement and interpretation is unambiguous. For example, if improved access to social services is adopted as an indicator it must be clear to all what is meant by 'access'. Increasing office hours may not really improve access if the office is still located in town a long distance from most potential clients. The indicators may include subjective judgements on progress (and people may have different perceptions) but the source of these judgements should be clear.

- **Credible** – there must be a reasonable case for the view that changes in the selected indicators are related, either directly or indirectly, to the project intervention.

- **Consistent** – in order to identify long term change it is important that the same indicators are measured over a long period. However, as project priorities and objectives change or there is a greater recognition of particular unanticipated impacts, indicators should be revised, with possibly some being replaced by more relevant ones.

- **Easy to collect** – it must be feasible to collect information on the chosen indicators within a reasonable time and at a reasonable cost.

Selecting Indicators

For a comprehensive monitoring and evaluation system, it is necessary to have indicators that show the project's progress in delivering its outputs, achieving its objectives and contributing to its goal: i.e. indicators of effort, effect and change are all needed (see Table 3).

It is usually much easier to identify appropriate indicators for outputs than it is for objectives and goals. As a result many monitoring and evaluation systems use indicators dominated by quantitative measures of output and do not develop adequate impact indicators. There are a number of factors which make it more difficult to find appropriate indicators of change:

- As a project moves from inputs to outputs, outcomes and impact, the influence of external factors beyond the scope of the project becomes increasingly felt. This makes it more difficult to be confident that changes in the indicator are necessarily caused by the project.

- Although the project may plan to bring about particular changes, its actual impact is likely to include unexpected elements, which were not considered in the planning stage and are not reflected in the initial indicators. In contrast, the outputs can be planned from the start of the project, which makes it relatively simple to find indicators.

- The impact of the project may be perceived very differently by different stakeholders. For example, if the project staff arrange visits to a demonstration farm by farmers, it may anticipate that the most important result will be the farmers' adoption of new techniques. However, the farmers may see the network of local farmers established through the visit as a valuable result. At times project impacts may even be contradictory for different stakeholders as a benefit for one may have negative consequences for another.

- Impact may take a longer time than expected to occur and become visible, thus straining the usefulness of indicators to capture this change.

In order to ensure that the monitoring and evaluation system remains both participatory and manageable, it is useful to reflect on who will identify the indicators, when indicators should be selected, and the number of indicators which should be used.

Who Selects Indicators?

It is very important that the process of selecting indicators is participatory. The major stakeholders, especially the intended beneficiaries, must contribute to the selection of indicators as they will have the best idea of what changes they hope to see as a result of the project.

At times different stakeholders take different views on what is an appropriate indicator, especially for indicators of effect or change. Roche (1999: 43) gives the example of an income-generating project, where a major indicator of success for the women involved was that they could now buy larger cooking pots. This enabled them to take fuller part in social and religious celebrations which increased their standing in the social network. An indicator like this could only arise from the project participants and it would not have been considered by the NGO involved. Such locally derived indicators which are bound up in the local context may make little sense to external observers unless the rationale behind them is explained to them. Equally, indicators favoured by project managers, such as an increase in household income, may make little sense to the project participants. They may know that any increased contribution from their efforts may be offset by their husband's putting in less, so any indicator must take account of the women's control over resources.

These examples also illustrate the point that indicators must be gender sensitive. Women and men may take contrasting views of project outputs and the effect and impact of them may be very different. Men may see that a well has been completed once they have contributed their labour to build it, whereas women, who have to collect water, may only see it as finished when it is fully operational and they can all use it.

When Should Indicators be Selected?

The monitoring and evaluation system must be considered from the planning stage and appropriate indicators of effort, effect and change should be drawn up at the start of the project, in consultation with the stakeholders. However, this set of indicators must be open to change through the life of the project.

Sometimes new indicators will have to be selected as a result of failings in existing indicators:

- It may prove impossible or too expensive to collect reliable data on the indicator. In this case, it may be possible to find a proxy indicator to provide the required evidence.

- Changes in the environment in which the project is operating may make an indicator redundant. For example, if the enrolment level in schools is taken as an indicator of household well-being, this may show nothing about the work of the project if the government abolishes school fees during the project.

- The relationship between the indicator and the project activities may not work as anticipated. This is particularly a danger if the project participants have not been fully consulted on the choice of indicators which are based on expectations of their behaviour. For example, increased consumption may be used as an indicator of increased income but people may first use the extra income to pay off debts. As a result there may be no visible change in consumption despite the people's income increasing.

It is essential to differentiate between shortcomings in the indicators and shortcomings in the project. If an indicator is not showing the expected changes because the project is not working out as planned, the response should be to ensure there are changes to the project (see Chapter 8), not changing indicators. Recall that indicators are only signs towards project progress. If the sign is pointing in an unexpected direction because that is where the project has gone, it is doing its work and should not be rejected.

New indicators may also be required in the light of participant's experience of the project and to monitor its unexpected consequences. A list of indicators drawn up before the project starts will only be able to pick up effects and changes which were thought of at the time. Few, if any, projects work out exactly according to plan, and it is common to find that the project activities may have results which were never anticipated. If the monitoring and evaluation system is to include such results, it is necessary to introduce new indicators to track these changes.

This may be particularly important in the case of negative impacts caused by the project. These are very unlikely to have been planned in advance, but inevitably, social development will not only have positive effects. In particular, improving the well-being of one group may cause a decline for others. For example, if a gas supply is introduced for an urban area, this may greatly improve the lives of households who can now cook on a cheap clean fuel. However, it may also destroy the businesses of many charcoal sellers, whose market will have disappeared. Such changes need to be monitored to ensure that project's overall impact is positive.

New indicators may also be required as the project participants develop a new understanding of their situation and the social development that is occurring. Roche (1999: 50) gives a helpful example of this:

> 'The way in which people's own indicators of poverty change over time is an important element in understanding how their needs, attitudes and values evolve. For example, when exploring changes in women's situation, CYSD in India found that women stressed that the main difficulty they had faced before the project was male dominance and the subordinate role of females. But these women had not considered this as a problem when the project first started. Their involvement with CYSD and their changing self-analysis had led them to this understanding. The fact that the women's indicators of change had evolved was an important indicator in itself that the project's efforts to change awareness and perceptions has borne fruit.'

Therefore, in a participatory monitoring and evaluation system, it is not sufficient to operate with a set of indicators that have all been chosen in advance. The initial set of indicators must be chosen in a participatory way and the system must allow it to be revised in the light of events and experience. Roche has helpfully summarised the qualities of such indicators using the acronym SPICED (see Table 6 below).

The Number of Indicators

A critical question concerns the number of indicators which a project might need in order for it to be able to measure the effect and impact of its activities. It is important that the set of indicators is restricted. Many organisations have found that project staff often respond

Table 6: *SPICED indicators (Roche 1999: 49)*

Subjective	Informants have a special position or experience that gives them unique insights which may yield a very high return on the investigator's time. In this sense, what may be seen by others as anecdotal becomes critical data because of the source's value.
Participatory	Indicators should be developed together with those best placed to assess them. This means involving a project's ultimate beneficiaries, but it can also mean involving local staff and other stakeholders.
Interpreted and communicable	Locally defined indicators may not mean much to other stakeholders, so they often need to be explained.
Cross-checked and compared	The validity of assessments needs to be cross-checked, by comparing different indicators and progress, and by using different informants, methods, and researchers.
Empowering	The process of setting and assessing indicators should be empowering in itself and allow groups and individuals to reflect critically on their changing situation.
Diverse and disaggregated	There should be a deliberate effort to seek out different indicators from a range of groups, especially men and women. This information needs to be recorded in such a way that these differences can be assessed over time.

to the challenge of monitoring and evaluation by creating large numbers of indicators, without regard for the effort involved in managing them. The list of indicators must take into account the resources available to collect the required information. It is better to assess effect and impact with a smaller number of relevant and manageable indicators, which offer the prospect of some understanding of the change that has taken place, rather than to be overwhelmed by an unmanageable and over ambitious set.

In any project the number of indicators used should decline as the project moves from output, to outcome, to impact. In a project with a well constructed project framework, if the indicators of output are and specific and relevant, they should be the basis for one or two broader indicators of outcome and then a general indicator of impact.

Developing a Process for Selecting Indicators

It is essential that the process of selecting indicators should be participatory and involve a range of key stakeholders. The first steps need to be taken during the planning stage of the project, when the monitoring and evaluation system is being designed. After the initial identification of indicators, they should be regularly reviewed and where necessary changed. The process may involve a series of workshops throughout the project as follows:

Activity	Objectives	Main participants
Initial workshop	To raise key questions To suggest indicators	Project beneficiaries Project staff Donor representatives
Operationalise indicators	To work out how suggested indicators would operate in practice – e.g. how will information be collected? To prepare list of indicators with associated data collection methods	Project staff in consultation with beneficiaries
Indicators workshop	To produce list of agreed indicators for project	Project participants Project staff Donor
Annual review of indicators	To look at how useful indicators have proved over period To agree on changes to indicator set	Project participants Project staff Donors

These do not need to be stand alone workshops but they may be part of other planning and monitoring workshops or project reviews. The main point is that the issue of indicators is openly discussed and an appropriate set is agreed.

CHAPTER 6
Data Collection

Selecting which data is required for monitoring and evaluation is only the first step towards an effective monitoring and evaluation system. This chapter is concerned with finding appropriate methods for gathering the information needed to show changes in the indicators.

There is a wide range of instruments or tools which are commonly used for collecting monitoring and evaluation data, some of which are introduced in this chapter. These include:

- Secondary sources
- Interviews with groups and individuals
- Formal surveys
- Participatory Rapid Appraisal (PRA) methods often using diagrams and maps
- Other methods such as participant observation and technical surveys.

Before looking at the details of particular methods, we look at some basic principles that will help to determine the choice of appropriate tools to use.

Choosing Data Collection Tools

It has been observed that often organisations take more care in selecting indicators than they do in working out how they will collect the required data (Simister 2000). An indicator is useless, if it is based on data that cannot be collected in practice. Given the wide range of instruments available for gathering information, it is important to make an appropriate choice among them, to ensure that the best tools are used for the job.

There are a number of factors which must be taken into account when deciding how to collect data for monitoring and evaluation:

- **The nature of the project** – the project's goal, activities, size and location will all affect how information should be gathered. For example, a large project involving thousands of participants scattered over a wide area will require different methods from a small project focused on development within one community. Different approaches are likely to be needed for a capacity building project and a local infrastructure project.

- **The type of indicators involved** – some methods are more suited to gathering quantitative than qualitative data and vice versa.

- **The time frame involved** – if one is looking to monitor changes which may occur from day to day, a diary may be useful. If one can only expect to see change over a longer period a semi-structured interview may be more appropriate.

- **The time available** – this may be of critical importance during evaluations, which often take place over a short time period.

- **The people available** – different tools require different skills to use them. Some tools may not be practical if there are insufficient people available to work with them. In particular, it may be difficult to find skilled facilitators for using qualitative methods extensively.

- **The funds available** – different tools will cost different amounts to use. A community meeting may involve a number of visits to the community for setting it up. The resultant costs of transport, staff time and subsistence may make it very expensive compared to a formal survey completed in one visit. The cost of analysis for the latter may be larger.

- **People's interest in participating** – an instrument that makes high demands of the time of project participants or other stakeholders will not be feasible if people are not willing to give the time. This is likely to be a problem with more participatory methods. People's willingness to take part will be increased if the project takes a participatory approach from the outset. In this case, the project may be largely 'owned' by the stakeholders who will have an interest in gathering information about it.

- **The purpose of data collection** – the appropriate tools will depend on the focus of monitoring or evaluation. Systems which are focused strongly on ensuring accountability to project participants and learning within the project may tend to use more qualitative, participatory methods, than those where the emphasis is on ensuring accountability to headquarters and donors. In any evaluation, the focus of the terms of reference will set the tone for the evaluation. This will be important for the evaluators in deciding which tools to use.

The relationship between some of these factors and different data collection methods is summarised in Box 7.

Any monitoring system or evaluation exercise should use a range of instruments for gathering data to ensure that findings are triangulated (see Chapter 4). Ideally for any indicator, the information required to show changes will come from a variety of sources.

A wide range of people may be involved in producing information for monitoring and evaluation depending on the methods used. The responsibility for recording and collating

Box 7: *Choosing data collection methods (Adapted from Marsden et al. 1994: 132)*

Data collection method	Requirements for use and analysis				Characteristics of data	Purpose of analysis
	Cost	Time	Expertise	Accuracy		
Focus group discussions	✓	✓✓✓	✓✓✓	✓	Difficult to organise groups but direct flow of information	Monitor development process, planning, **not** control or accountability
Individual interviews	✓✓	✓✓	✓✓✓	✓✓	Both quantitative and qualitative, data depends on quality of interviewers	Accountability up, planning, control, **not** accountability down
Formal social surveys	✓✓✓	✓✓	✓✓✓	✓✓✓	Quantitative data	Accountability up, planning, control
Participatory techniques	✓	✓✓✓	✓✓	✓✓	Views of participants but time consuming. Part of development process	Accountability down, impact, **not** control
Observation	✓	✓✓	✓✓✓	✓✓✓	Depends on person making observation	Impact, accountability up, **not** control, accountability down
Participant observation	✓	✓✓✓	✓✓	✓✓	Good for understanding target groups and impact	Information, planning, impact, **not** control, accountability up/down
Secondary information	✓	✓	✓	n/a	Complementary, saves collecting duplicate data, good for comparison	Planning **not** accountability, impact
Technical/ geographical surveys	✓✓✓	✓	✓✓✓	✓✓✓	Good for physical data, assumes relevance	Information, planning, account-ability up, impact, **not** accountability down, control
Financial audit	✓✓	✓✓	✓✓✓	✓✓✓	Good for financial assessment	Accountability, control, planning, **not** impact

the data ready for analysis is likely to lie with either the project staff, in the case of monitoring, or the evaluation team during an evaluation. As pointed out in Chapters 2 and 3, monitoring data should be collected systematically throughout the project. The monitoring records will be the first source of data for an evaluation, which will then supplement it with additional information depending on the terms of reference and focus of the evaluation.

In addition to any information collected through the efforts of the project staff using data collection tools, it is also essential to ensure that other opportunities for data gathering are used. Some information may be gathered through minimal changes to regular practices, for example, adding a section to project visit reports to note observations relating to indicators. Other information will require special activities such as meetings, interviews, and surveys. Any data gathering exercise may use more than one method. In particular, observations of people's behaviour and social interactions during interviews and meetings can provide helpful triangulation of what they are saying. For example, if a person claims to take a participatory approach to management but is observed to dominate the conversation to the exclusion of others, this will call into question his or her claim (see participant observation below).

Some information may be shared with the project without any requests being made – e.g. when a participant visits the project office and in conversations says what changes the project has brought. This unsolicited information may be particularly important as it may be more likely to reflect the most meaningful changes (If you ask somebody what difference the project has made, they may try to think up something to please you). This information may provide very helpful data to triangulate the data gathered through more formal means.

Improving the Quality of Information

The information produced by the monitoring and evaluation system should be used in decision making. It is therefore essential that the information is of high quality. It is easy to fill in forms or produce opinions that can be taken as data for monitoring and evaluation purposes. However, inaccurately recorded answers in questionnaires or interviews which are only partially written up long after the event, are not a sound basis for revising a project's current operations or future planning.

Triangulating data by using a mix of methods and sources is a very important technique for improving the reliability, validity and credibility of information (see Chapter 4). However, whatever range of methods and systems are put in place, they will be reliant on the ongoing support of project staff for their day to day operation. This is especially true of monitoring, which is carried out by staff as part of their routine management of the project.

The quality of the data produced by the system will critically depend on the project staff and the institutional context. Increasing the interest of the staff in the collection of information is likely to increase the quality of the information they gather. Where they are simply required to gather data to submit in reports to another office, they are unlikely to have much interest in it and may pass on mistakes and confusing data uncritically. The more information is used by staff in the field, the greater interest they will have in ensuring that it is

Figure 8: *The criteria for achieving high quality data collection* (Source: Simister 2000)

Quality of information	Requirements of field staff	Institutional requirements
LOW QUALITY ↑ ↓ **HIGH QUALITY**	• Data collection skills • Motivation • Understanding of how monitoring data is used • Confidence in monitoring as a non-threatening process • Opportunities to comment on data / analyses • Reporting of own experiences/knowledge lying outside the formal monitoring system • Opportunity to analyse/use data at field level	• Training • Supervision • Specific training on the uses of monitoring data • Feedback of analyses / results to the field • Positive responses to the reporting of errors / mistakes • Systems to encourage the two-way flow of information • Review mechanisms • Some decentralisation of decision making • Establishment of informal channels of communication • Reassurance of field staff that their experience, knowledge and opinions are valued • Mechanisms to allow field staff some input into the design of monitoring systems • Decentralisation of decision-making • Organisational culture encouraging participation

accurate. It is also vital that the monitoring data is not seen as threatening to field staff, especially when it is concerned with shortcomings in the project. Otherwise, staff will have an interest in suppressing data which reveals problems. Figure 8 shows these and other criteria for ensuring that field staff produce high quality information.

Sampling

Whatever data collection methods are used and however participatory the approach, it is likely to be impractical to consult every project stakeholder (direct and indirect) during monitoring and evaluation. It will therefore be necessary to make decisions about who to involve in data collection, i.e. to select a sample of the stakeholders.

Before choosing a sample, it is important to define the *sampling frame* – the overall set of people who could be consulted during a particular data exercise. The appropriate sampling frame will depend on the units of analysis that are being used (see Chapter 4):

- The whole population of a community – where the project affects everybody or it is important to see the differences between the target population of the intervention and others;

- A section of the population – e.g. women or youths;

- Every household within the community;

- A number of communities – possibly to compare those within the project area and others outside it.

Sample size

A critical decision is to decide the size of the sample required. If you do not talk to enough people, the results of the monitoring or evaluation may be skewed towards the views of a few individuals, who are not representative of the overall population. Increasing the sample size will increase the accuracy of the picture produced but it will also cost more in time and money (not only for data collection but also for analysis). Beyond a certain size, the improved accuracy gained by increasing the sample size will be small compared to the additional costs incurred.

It is essential to bear in mind the principle of achieving optimal ignorance at this point (see Chapter 4) in order to achieve the appropriate sample size. Where statistical analysis will be used, the sample size can be calculated using standard methods (see Nichols 1991). In other circumstances, it will be a matter of judgement and experience to weigh up the gain to be made by increasing the sample size against the costs involved.

There are many ways of selecting a sample from the overall set and they fall into two main categories: random sampling and non-random sampling. Some of these are outlined below. For more details see Nichols (1991).

Random Sampling

- **Simple random sampling:** a group of people are selected at random from a complete list of a given population (the sampling frame). If the overall population is 250 and you decide to sample 20%, 50 people must be selected. This could be done by giving each member of the population a number. Put the 250 pieces of paper with all the numbers into a bag, and select 50 of the pieces of paper. You then interview the people whose numbers correspond with those taken out of the bag. Alternatively many calculators can generate random numbers and you can use them to make your selection rather than folding pieces of paper.

- **Stratified random sampling:** the overall population is broken down into non-overlapping sub-groups (e.g. by gender, ethnic group, wealth, location etc.) and a random sample is taken from each sub-group. This makes it possible to ensure that each of the sub-groups is fully represented – e.g. if 30% of households are headed by women, 30% of the overall sample should be taken from the set of female headed households.

- **Cluster sampling:** the geographical area covered by the overall population is divided into segments or clusters, possibly by villages or neighbourhoods. First a random sample is taken to select clusters and within each cluster a random sample of respondents is identified. This may reduce the costs and time involved in data collection as it ensures the respondents are in a limited number of small areas rather than scattered across a much wider area.

- **Staged sampling:** this is similar to cluster sampling, where there is sampling within sampling. For example, if a project has many offices each serving many communities, the first level of random sampling may select the office to look at, a second level will select the communities and a third level may select the individual households to be interviewed.

- **Random walk:** Where you know the overall size of the population but you may not know the names or addresses, it may be easiest simply to take a random walk through the community, taking turns (left, right etc.) and choosing individual houses at random – possibly using dice. If you are confident that there is no pattern differentiating different locations in the community, it may be easier simply to go to households at a regular interval. The size of the interval will depend on the required sample size – if it is 20% you should interview at every fifth house, 25% every fourth house, etc. This technique can also be used when you do not know precisely the size of the sampling frame.

Non-random Sampling

- **Quota sampling:** Given information about the overall population, a certain number of people (organisations or communities – depending on the units of analysis) from different categories are approached for interview or whatever method is to be used. This might be based on gender, ethnic group, communities inside or outside the project area etc. The selection of people involved may be made on the basis of the first come first served, the most feasible to reach in the time available. Interviews continue until the quota is reached. This method is open to the danger of 'tarmac bias' or other forms of bias where the people involved might be those living in the most accessible places or those best known to the project staff. This can be counteracted by ensuring that more remote communities are included and ensuring it is not always the same people involved.

- **Snowball or chain sampling:** This is a common method in qualitative interviews, where the respondent is asked to suggest who else it might be appropriate to approach for interview. This can be helpful in dealing with sensitive topics or interviewing a minority whom it might not otherwise be easy to identify.

Using Tools

Whichever tools are used there are areas where the appropriate behaviour by project staff can make the exercise more successful. These are highlighted in Table 7 opposite.

Secondary Sources

Secondary sources of data should be the first place to look for monitoring and evaluation data. Secondary sources are other organisations which produce information for their own purposes that may be useful for monitoring and evaluation. These might include government statistics, UN reports, surveys carried out by other NGOs or development organisations, academic literature, etc. Where somebody else has already collected information which is not only reliable, valid and credible but also relevant for monitoring the effort, effect or change caused by your project, then use it. There is no point in repeating the work that others have already done.

Interview Techniques

Many of the tools involve some form of interview techniques and the following are some general guidelines to various forms of interviews. These include informal interviews, semi-structured interviews, community group interviews and focus group interviews.

The numbers of people involved range from a whole community to a single key informant, or person who you think will have relevant information concerning the

How big should interview groups be?
There is a link between group size and participation.

3-6 people	everybody speaks
7-10 people	almost everybody speaks
11-20 people	5-6 people speak a lot
	3-4 others join in occasionally
	others keep quiet
more than 20	3-4 people dominate
	little or no participation

Table 7: *Tools and staff behaviour*

Approach	• Use an appropriate form of transport. It may be much better to walk in a village (an advantage of this is that you may observe more things than would be possible when travelling by car). • Do not go in large numbers. Two in a team is often best. • Be sensitive to the fact that people may be suspicious of your motives for collecting data. • Be considerate of the daily work schedule, seasonal activity, work habits, climate etc. Sometimes discussions can be successful if you can walk to the field and discussions centre around ongoing agricultural activities. • Make sure that you make appointments where possible and do not expect people to drop everything if you arrive unexpectedly.
Warm Up	• Don't go directly into the subject at hand. First greet the person/ people appropriately. Always treat the people/person with respect. Do not talk to people from your vehicle if you are in one. • Tell them why you are here and why you wish to talk to them. Be honest and open. • Make sure the context you are in is conducive to an interview. • Ask permission if you want to take notes, record or take photos.
Dialogue	• Be natural and relaxed. • In qualitative interviews let discussion flow and mix up your questions. Be flexible. • Do not be aggressive or defensive. • In qualitative interviews, if the person/ people you are talking to are unable to answer the question, rephrase the question rather than suggesting answers for them! (This should not occur in formal surveys if they are tested properly.) • Always use plain and understandable language. • Be culturally sensitive.
Departure	• Do not end a discussion abruptly as this can seem rude. Thank them for the time they have given you and depart with the proper local farewell.
Recording	• Always record the date, place of interview and, unless the interview is confidential, the name of those involved. • After the interview jot down notes, if you did not take them during the interview. • It is up to you to assess if the situation is suitable for taking notes in front of the group or individual you are interviewing.

indicators. Key informants can be very helpful in providing a rich source of knowledge which may have been overlooked and they may sometimes open up a new perspective on the projects' effect and impact.

Whatever form of interview is used, the following points should be considered when deciding on the questions to ask:

- The wording must be very clear so that the questions cannot be misinterpreted – e.g. an answer to a question such as 'How did you find the staff at the health centre?' could be either, 'They were very polite and helpful,' or 'I had to go their house as it was the evening.'

- Do not ask leading questions that suggest what answer is expected – e.g. 'Do you think the service is useful?' A question phrased in this way will suggest the answer should be 'Yes'. It would be better to ask, 'What do you think of the service?'

- Only ask one question at a time as this will make it more likely that you will receive clear and concise answers – e.g. 'What sort of seeds did you buy through the project last year and what yield did they produce?' These two points of the types of seed bought and then the quality of the yield should be dealt with through separate questions.

Informal Interviews

These aim to elicit information through conversations between interviewers and respondents. They explore, broadly, the views, experiences and values of the respondent by giving the interviewer freedom to pursue issues as they arise. Because of their informal nature, few notes, if any, should be taken. You need to have skill to be able to bring out information that may not have been volunteered in a more formal setting.

There are limitations to this interviewing technique. They can be very time consuming as conversations can drift form point to point and become difficult to control. Information relating to broad issues from a number of individuals can be difficult to collate and draw conclusions from.

Topic Focused or Semi Structured Interviews

These make use of an interview guide to ensure that the main topics are covered. From this, the interviewer develops his/her questions and format to fit the individual respondent. There is no time limit on the response to each topic and the pursuit of particular topics of interest is allowed.

A topic focused / semi-structured interview can be repeated by the same interviewer but with different respondents and in this way a range of responses is obtained.

Semi-structured or open-ended interviews are when there are lists of questions to be asked. However, they differ from the traditional structured interview by:

- Having open ended questions which allow expansion of points raised

- Having a flexible sequence of questions which allow for interviewer discretion

- Leaving room for additional questions to be asked.

A disadvantage of open-ended methods and semi-structured interviews is that areas where more in depth probing would be useful are not always picked up by the interviewer.

Community Interviews

These are open for all members of a community or village. Good planning is important if they are to be successful. When conducting these interviews remember:

- The use of structured interview guides should be standard practice. Without these, conversations can easily drift. Language should be kept simple and controversial, political or culturally sensitive questions should be avoided;

- A few carefully selected and representative communities should be interviewed;

- Interviews should be selected at times when the majority of people within the community can attend. Different groups, in particular women and men may only be able to come at different times. Remember to fit into other people's timetables and not what suits you;

> In Indonesia the best time for interviewing is between 4pm, after prayer and before evening meal, when people are in their homes. However, in Peru's highlands, the best time for interviewing is in the morning, before the day's activities get underway.

- It may be necessary to hold separate meetings for different sections of the community, e.g. separate meetings for men and women, or youth and elders. This will ensure that the views of a broad cross-section of community are heard;

- A team of interviewers (two is best) is preferable to an individual, as conducting a meeting between many people and taking extensive notes is demanding and time consuming. Multiple notes can be better than just one set and also more rounded questioning can be achieved by a team of questioners. If a team is used, make sure that it is not too over-powering;

- Participation by a balanced representation of those attending is essential. Prominent individuals should not dominate. It is legitimate for the interviewer to invite people every so often to answer the question. By doing so some of those who would otherwise not have answered are given the chance;

- Aggregate data can be gained through these interviews. Other people should then be asked to verify the data provided and reasonably accurate estimates can be obtained;

- Meetings after the interview should be considered, especially for those who felt inhibited to speak more publicly about their ideas. The time and place for such a meeting should be clearly stated at the end of the interview.

Focus Group Interviews

Focus group interviews differ from community interviews in that they use a smaller number of people who have been selected according to the contribution they are expected to make.

Focus groups can provide a good means of analysing how people interact and discuss issues as they rely on interactions between the members of the group and not simply interaction between the researchers' questions and the participants' responses.

> **Focus Groups**
> - It is a free discussion
> - They can be used to explore sensitive issues
> - There are no right or wrong statements
> - Need to cross check information

The success of focus groups will depend on the culture in which they are being used and the topic being investigated. If the subject is one which cannot be discussed in public, there may be very limited interaction between people in a focus group, unless the people all know each other very well. In these circumstances, it may be better to use individual interviews.

Focus groups can be useful in order to collect a large amount of data in a relatively short amount of time, as they combine elements of both participant observation and interviewing.

Several points to be aware of in focus groups are:

- As sub topics are to be explored in depth the use of a short checklist is all that is required to allow for expansion on the issues raised.

- The optional number of participants is between six and ten in order to facilitate useful conversation and allow all to have their say without making them feel obliged to talk continuously.

> Remember that members of the group should be from the same social and economic strata to make discussion easier and to get rid of any status barriers.

- Meetings should be held in privacy with seating arranged to facilitate maximum interaction among participants. The use of tables and chairs (if there are any) arranged in a semi circle is recommended. Make sure that as interviewer you are not the only person sitting on a chair as this puts a barrier between you and the focus group.

- Focus group discussions should be no longer than two hours.

- Participants should be told that they are part of an informal discussion, that all can participate, and that all ideas are welcome.

- To limit discussion to the required areas of interest, the interviewer should budget time for each topic accordingly.

- Awareness of the existence of group pressure is important. This can be minimised by encouraging the expression of diverse views and perspectives.

Surveys

Formal surveys are often used when the majority of information required is quantitative or lends itself to quantitative analysis. For example, if the project is concerned with addressing food security, it may be important to find out what types of food are available to people, the prices they are paying for it, and the volume they are consuming. Here there is only space to give very basic guidelines for setting up formal surveys using questionnaires. For more details see Pratt and Loizos (1992).

Most surveys involve a set of closed questions with a list of possible responses. The survey is prepared on a form and the interviewer simply has to ask the set questions exactly as written and record the answers, often by ticking boxes. The answers can usually be coded in some way for easy analysis by computer. It is important that formal surveys are carried out with a representative sample of the population, usually a random sample (see above). The number of respondents will tend to be considerably larger than would be considered for other tools. Where formal statistical methods are to be used in the analysis, it is possible to calculate the minimum sample size required. It is essential that the number of respondents is at least as large as this minimum in order for the statistical results to be valid.[1]

Once a survey is running, it can capture a lot of routine information quite quickly using less skilled people, often known as enumerators, than other interviews. The enumerators need to be able to approach people and encourage them to answer the questions, but they do not need to ask follow up questions or record complex answers. Surveys necessarily record a very simplified picture of what is happening.

However, if a survey is to be of any use it has to be carefully designed to ensure that the data recorded is reliable and valid. Questions must be phrased very carefully to avoid ambiguity and the enumerators must be clear about how they should record responses. If there are any problems in the record, it will be very difficult to detect, as answers are likely to consist only of tick boxes, numbers and lists. Therefore, before carrying out a full survey it is good practice to prepare the questionnaire and try it out on some people. This trial (or pilot) survey will often reveal unexpected points of confusion that should be tackled before the main survey takes place. The box overleaf gives an illustration of poor questionnaire design and how some of the issues can be addressed.

---

[1] See Rowntree 1988 or Frinton 1995 for basic guidance on using statistical methods.

It may be appropriate to include some aspects of a formal survey questionnaire in other interviews, or append other qualitative interview questions to a formal survey. In a largely qualitative interview asking some standard questions about household structure or respondents' use of a service may help to ensure that the interviews are representative. For example, your results may be biased if you find you are talking mainly to women from female headed households.

Likewise a formal questionnaire may contain prompting questions – why? how? – which ask for more explanation of an answer. The danger is that this places greater demands on the enumerator to record responses carefully and it also makes analysis more difficult. In a large survey, qualitative, unstructured responses may be very interesting but, if they cannot be analysed properly, they may not be of much use. It may then be better to separate the two methods and carry out a limited number of qualitative interviews to give more detail to the picture given by the formal survey.

A poorly designed questionnaire

QI   Do you travel a lot outside the village?

[The interviewer has jumped straight into the task without a word of explanation or introduction. This is bound to seem abrupt, if not rude. The question itself is a very vague question. What is 'a lot', and what will be learned from the answer, whether it is 'yes' or 'no'?]

Q2   How do you travel?

[This question will encourage a very general answer, and possibly some confusion. If the listener is thinking about the next village, one kind of answer will emerge; but if they are thinking of a market town 50 kilometres away, then another will apply.]

Q3   When do you travel?

[Although this question looks specific, it can elicit all kinds of answers: 'When I have to.' 'When someone offers me a lift.' 'When I have something to sell.' 'When I must buy something.' 'If a child is sick.' The question merges times and motives in the word 'when' and gives no clue as to which kind of answer is intended.]

Q4   Would you use the new minibus service more if it were cheap?

[Another vague question, and it is hypothetical, as well. It invites the answer 'yes' and little more.]

Q5   Who else in your household also travels outside the village?

[It is much better to ask each member of the household about their actual behaviour, separately. The only excuse for a question in this form would be a drastic shortage of time or money. It is possible that a male household head would give answers about his wife and children which carried implications about his status and authority; these answers would not necessarily be a reliable guide to what really happens.]

A more thoughtfully designed questionnaire

Introduction: Hello. My names is ... and I am working with NGO. NGO has been involved in setting up a minibus service for this area and we are trying to understand if this is meeting people's transport requirements. Could you please spare me a little time – about 15 minutes – to answer some simple questions about your use of transport? I'm asking people from every house in the village. There are no right or wrong answers to the questions.

[These introductory remarks should inform interviewees exactly what is going on and should set them at their ease.]

Q1   In the last 3 months, you may have travelled outside the village. I want to write down all the times you did this, and for what purpose starting, with the most recent trip.

A1   the place ....   the reason ....

A2   the place ....   the reason ....

A3   the place ....   the reason ....

Continue on separate sheet if necessary

[By choosing actual, recent behaviour, and by eliciting an open-ended number of examples, this question and the following questions avoid the vague generalities which might have resulted from the first questionnaire.]

Q2   When you travelled to (place from A1) how did you travel? Tick one of the following:

By foot   ❑   On an animal   ❑   By bicycle   ❑   By motorbike   ❑

By truck   ❑   By minibus   ❑   By large bus   ❑   By car   ❑

Other (specify)...

(Repeat for all the answers to Q1)

Q3   How much did it cost to travel to (place from A1)?

(Repeat for all the answers to Q1)

Q4   How much is it worth to you to be able to go by minibus once a week to the town XYZ, and come back on the same day?

        Not more than 50 pesos ❑   From 105-120 pesos   ❑

        From 55-75 pesos   ❑   Over 125 pesos

        From 80-100 pesos   ❑   (state amount)...............................

[This question is hypothetical, and so the answers must be treated with caution. They are compared with actual prices being paid, either in this community or a similar one]

Source: adapted from Pratt and Loizos 1992: 89-91

Participatory Rapid Appraisal Tools

This is a family of tools, which, as the name suggests, aims to involve a wide range of stake-holders. A distinctive feature of all of these tools is that they are not aiming simply to collect data but also to conduct preliminary analysis of findings in the field. Information is shared in a group setting and then discussed to produce some consensus. This process requires careful facilitation as the focus should be on enabling participants to raise the questions and provide answers for themselves rather than collecting information using predetermined questions brought from outside.

Many of the tools make extensive use of visual aids such as pictures, diagrams, charts and maps. This makes them more accessible to participants who are not literate or are not used to reading and writing. It also produces a physical output which belongs to the participants. It is not uncommon to see the pictures and diagrams produced by PRAs displayed by communities for a long time after the meeting which produced them. The discussions and conclusions reached through the exercise are therefore more likely to remain in participants minds for longer than when the sole record in the form of notes is taken away.

The tools listed here are only a selection of those available and new ones are being added all the time. It is expected that the tools should be flexible and they will need to be adapted for different contexts. Further details about PRA and these tools can be found in Slocum et al. (1995), Mikkelsen (1995), Gosling and Edwards (1995).

Mapping

- **Social Network Mapping** – A map to show the pattern of social and economic linkages, either between communities or within a community, such as those which result from the exchange of materials or services.

- **Community Mapping** – A schematic drawing of an area, used to identify the location and types of resources used by a community, from the perspective of its inhabitants.

Ranking

- **Matrix Ranking** – A matrix used to structure perceptions and opinions of informants so that individual, group or household criteria or qualities can be ranked in order of priority.

- **Pairwise Ranking** – A way of helping a community to rank and prioritise issues such as problems or preferences and, when utilised with different individuals or groups within the community, to become aware of the differences of opinions.

- **Wealth or Well-Being Ranking** – The purpose of this exercise is to highlight local perceptions on the definitions and the indicators of the different wealth groups within the community.

Schedules/Calendars

- **Daily Schedule** – A diagram to show an individual's patterns of labour over the course of a day. This usually shows the type and distribution of workload and enables a comparative analysis between men and women, young and old, domestic and agricultural roles etc.

- **Seasonal Calendar** – A chart used to identify, illustrate and compare key events and changes within a year, such as during the agricultural cycle. Multiple variables can be identified and compared within the calendar, such as cropping patterns, labour demands, food stocks, market prices and weather.

- **Time Line** – An illustration of key events in the life of an individual, household, community or organisation over a specified period of time in the past.

Matrices

- **Access to and Control of Resource**s – Picture Cards / Matrix – This simple tool identifies the different resources that men and women have access to and control over. It is useful for collecting information about the division of labour, cultural norms and power relations within households and groups.

- **Income Expenditure Balance Sheet** – An Income Expenditure Balance Sheet is a matrix to compare the available income of a household with its expenditure.

- **Livelihood Analysis** – This tool explores livelihoods by looking at proportions of total incomes and expenditures rather than requiring detail about monetary values. Total income or expenditure is represented in a pie or bar chart and divided proportionally according to sources of income and needs for expenditures.

- **Gender Division of Labour** – This tool provides detailed information about the division of labour by gender and its consequences within a household and may explain why men and women carry out certain tasks and not others. It can be particularly interesting when conducted alongside the exercise on access to and control over resources.

Diagrams

- **Venn Diagram** – A set of different size circles – each representing an institution – drawn to show the relationships between a community or household and the institutions that affect it.

- **Flow Chart** – A visual tool for tracking the flow of resources, benefits or negative effects in order to explore impacts of a project or a change. People, institutions, resources and so on are represented diagrammatically and arrows are drawn between them to indicate the flow or the linkages between entities.

Other

- **Testimonials** – A recorded narrative – delivered in the first person – of an individual's attitude to and experience of a particular situation or project.

- **Group Functioning (Three Star Game)** – This tool aims to enable a community (or a group within the community) that is running a project to measure the contribution of key people and activities to the functionality of the group. This allows people of the community to evaluate their own performance.

- **Story With A Gap** – The story teller describes the beginning and the end of a series of events; often associated with a problem faced by a community, organisation or household. The middle section of the story is purposely left out and participants fill in the gap with their own assessment of what should have happened in order to arrive at the end scenario described.

Other Tools

Some other tools which might be considered for gathering monitoring and evaluation data include:

- **Participant observation** – as a general technique, this involves observing the normal daily lives of beneficiaries and recording what is seen. This may include descriptions of social interactions (who talks to whom, who offers respect to whom, the manners people use to talk to others, group dynamics), behaviour (responses to events, use of power), etc. Such observations may be made by project staff living within the community or community members. In addition, observations can be made in parallel with any of the other techniques for data collection described here. This may be particularly helpful for identifying inconsistencies between what people say they do and what they do in practice.

- **Technical surveys** – these may provide technical assessments of the project's progress. For example, building work may need to be surveyed by an engineer to check that the appropriate quality of materials has been used and the building is structurally sound. Land use surveys, vegetation coverage or other outputs from geographical information systems (GIS) may be useful for assessing project impact. Such surveys may be very expensive and are only likely to be feasible for large projects. Although these techniques are not participatory, the information generated through them should be presented back to the project participants in an accessible form.

- **Financial audit** – most organisations will conduct a financial audit each year as part of the requirements of their constitution. Donors will often expect to see audited accounts each financial year. For most projects, it is therefore unlikely that a special audit will be required for monitoring and evaluation. In the case of projects involving large financial flows which may not appear in the organisations overall accounts, a separate financial audit may be appropriate – for example, in micro-finance interventions.

CHAPTER 7

Data Analysis

Once monitoring and evaluation data has been collected, it must be analysed if it is to provide useful information which will meet the requirements of the monitoring and evaluation system – to measure progress, ensure accountability to beneficiaries and donors, to advise on project revisions, and to provide lessons for stakeholders, and to assess the intervention's sustainable impact. Data analysis is the process of converting the raw 'information' collected into 'knowledge' that can be used for decision making and lesson learning (see Chapter 4). In this chapter, the process is described in more detail and some of the methods used for analysis are presented.

Steps in Data Analysis

The process of analysis includes a number of steps:

- **Review** – the whole range of data on the different indicators should be brought together and organised to show what information is available to give evidence of change in the three levels of indicators – effort, effect and change. The review should consider the reliability of each piece of evidence and resolve contradictions where possible. This may reveal gaps in the data which need to be filled before proceeding further.

- **Summarise** – using the results of this review the most reliable and important points of evidence showing effort, effect and change should be summarised. This summary will give an overview of the project's progress at the levels of outputs, outcomes and impact and the supporting evidence.

- **Interrogate** – various questions should now be asked and answers put forward. For example:
    Is the picture given in the summary a realistic one?
    Do stakeholders agree about the picture presented – is there consensus or conflict?
    What factors explain the success or failure of the project at each level – output,

outcome and impact?

Are there other external factors which should be taken into account?

Have appropriate indicators been used?

Have appropriate methods for collecting data been used?

- **Learn** – the summary of data and answers to questions should highlight lessons of what works and what does not work, in terms of activities, approaches and policies. These should be recorded.

- **Action** – the analysis should conclude with actions which are to be taken as a result of the lessons learnt. For monitoring purposes these may relate to revisions to the project's practice (new activities, revised outputs etc.) or to the monitoring system (new indicators, new data collection tools). These may be included in an evaluation, but in addition, an evaluation is likely to make recommendations about the overall project direction and aims, and even whether the project should continue or not.

The first three steps may be repeated until an agreed picture emerges from the data (see Figure 9 below). These three steps are the focus of this chapter. Learning and action are covered in more detail in Chapter 8 on data use.

Figure 9: *Process of analysis*

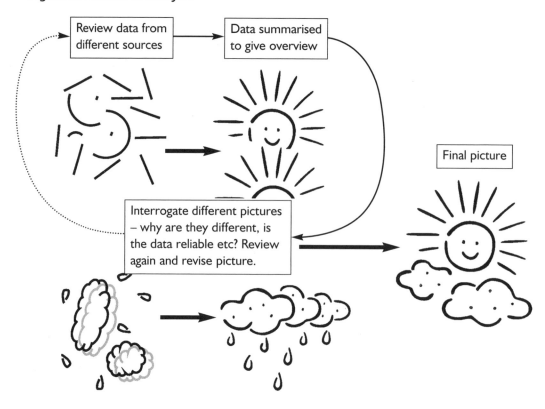

The following issues should be considered when planning data analysis:

- **Analyse at the field level** – as far as possible, people collecting data should be involved in analysis. If the people who are collecting data do not use it, they will have no interest in ensuring that it is accurate. If they do not understand why it is needed at all, except to keep headquarters happy, they may be less inclined to collect it at all.

- **Value should be added at every level** – it is very important that the process of analysis should take place at every level of the organisation(s) involved, from the field project to headquarters. Monitoring and evaluation data should never be passed on from one level to the next without analysis, as the potential usefulness of the information will be lost. In the past, because monitoring and evaluation systems have focused on ensuring accountability to donors, there has been a tendency for field staff to collect monitoring data that is demanded by headquarters but is of little use at the field level.

- **Analysis should be participatory** – the analysis of data should be a participatory exercise involving both project beneficiaries and staff. This can be done by open discussions or review meetings which aim to reach a consensus on the analysis which can be recorded. Both individual and collective memory will be important aspects of analysis and interpretation with different stakeholders playing a role in retrospectively drawing out the major conclusions on what has been the impact of a particular intervention. This role may not come easy and it is probable that a trial period will be needed to give all stakeholders and staff the opportunity to understand the exercise and to develop the skills necessary to play an active role.

- **Analysis should be regular** – analysis should take place regularly, ideally soon after information was collected. In particular, monitoring data should be analysed routinely rather than being saved for annual reports or the evaluation. The regularity of the meetings will be dictated by factors particular to the context and to the project, but almost certainly periodic exercises of verifying what is happening will take place every three months or so. A regular three-monthly half day exercise, which allows a project to develop an understanding of what is unfolding, is to be preferred to an annual review that may be overwhelmed by all the changes that may have taken place during the year.

- **Data should not be manipulated to produce 'right' answers** – qualitative processes of change, by definition, can often unfold slowly with the result that periodically the recording might lack substance. In such circumstances there is the danger that inaccurate recordings may be made or negative data ignored by staff anxious to see some progress.

- **The analysis will reflect different cultural contexts** – explanations and interpretations are expressions of people's culture, values and concerns. It will be important that the analysis brings out the values of the different stakeholders and examines and compares them. What is meant by 'success' and 'failure' will be influenced by language, culture and values. Assessing what constitutes 'change' may not be obvious, as both events and actions can be explained and interpreted differently.

Different Forms of Analysis

Remember that we are trying to establish a chain of evidence which relates what is happening in people's lives and the activities of the project. The analysis should pull together the evidence from the different data sources.

The analysis must refer to the baselines established at the start of the project, if they exist. Failing that it may look at the developments since the last review or evaluation. Otherwise, the analysis will be largely descriptive as it will be restricted to presenting a snapshot of how things are at the time of data collection rather than showing how things have changed.

There are many methods of data analysis available, more than can possibly be covered here. They can be divided into two forms, mirroring the broad division between quantitative and qualitative data. For more detail on qualitative analysis see Miles and Huberman (1994) and for quantitative analysis see Rowntree (1988) or Frinton (1995).

Qualitative Analysis

Much of qualitative analysis is concerned with reading and rereading the information gathered – interview reports, diagrams etc. The challenge is to develop a picture that is a reliable, valid and credible reflection of the underlying data. Given the large variety of sources and formats for qualitative data, there are no simple recipes for consistently achieving this. However, it is possible to suggest some broad techniques which may be helpful.

Within a set of qualitative data, there may be a vast range of interesting material. It is important to focus primarily on that which relates to the monitoring and evaluation task at hand. This can be done by linking the data to the set of indicators for the project – to go through all the information systematically and write down against each indicator what evidence there is for change (both positive and negative). As you go through the information mark off the points which you use.

After completing that process, highlight the other data which has not been used. For example, one interview may discuss the fact that crop yields have improved and that women are having to work harder to cope with the increased farm activity. The former may refer to an indicator (change in crop yields) but the latter may not refer to any indicators. However, this point should be highlighted as it is evidence of an unintended consequence of the project.

As the picture emerges from the data, it is essential that those involved in analysis refer back to the source documents (reports, diagrams etc.) to ensure that the picture is consistent with what is there. The first review will pick up some points, but there will be others which will be neglected. Subsequent reviews of the source data will bring forward other points. First impressions are not good enough.

Whatever particular method is used, a systematic approach must be adopted to ensure that the resultant analysis is reliable. If another person analysed the same data, would they come to the same conclusions? The process of analysis will inevitably involve some degree of interpretation of people's statements and views recorded in the data. To ensure that the analysis is valid, the interpretations must be reasonable and not biased to give a favourable view of the project.

In order to avoid such bias creeping in, it is very important that the analysis is considered by more than one person. If a participatory approach is being used, this should not need stating. However, where NGO staff work to tight deadlines, especially for donor reports, they may be tempted to prepare a report in isolation. Even if a fully participatory process is not adopted, the views of another person will act as a critical 'sanity check'.

As noted in Chapter 5, it may sometimes be appropriate to summarise some qualitative data in a quantitative form, which can then be analysed using quantitative methods. This can be done by coding particular responses to open questions. For example, if beneficiaries are routinely asked questions about the most important changes which have occurred as a result of the project, they may come out with a wide range of answers concerned with many areas of life, e.g. increased income, better health, no impact, etc. It may be possible to group their responses by these areas, e.g. income, health, education, nothing etc., and mark each one as positive, negative, neutral or no response. This will result in a table such as that shown below, which can then be analysed using quantitative methods.

	Category of impact			
Respondent	Income	Health	Education	No impact
1	+	+	+	
2				1
3	0	+	-	
4	-	-	+	
5	+	0	0	

It is important to note that a different table would have been produced using a formal survey as this would have required the categories of impact to be determined in advance before asking the questions. Using a qualitative approach, the categories of impact emerge through the process of data analysis.

Quantitative Analysis

Quantitative analysis may appear to be easier than qualitative. The raw data comes in a standard format and there are well developed routine methods for analysing it. These range from calculating simple totals, averages and percentages to sophisticated statistical methods which test the relationship between different variables.

In qualitative analysis, the choices of what to include and what significance to place on various items of data clearly lie with those carrying out the analysis. This is what makes it more difficult. In quantitative analysis, the same choices need to be made, but they tend to be pre-determined by the technical requirements of the methods being used.

In other words, many assumptions lie buried in the calculations and these need to be understood by those carrying out the analysis. Common assumptions concern the size of the sample related to the overall population, the random nature of the sample, the independence of different variables, etc. If the appropriate assumptions do not hold, the analysis will be invalid. Moreover, it is easy to make mistakes in calculations, which may be very hard to spot, especially when there are many steps in the analysis. The danger is that it is easy to generate numbers using quantitative analysis, but difficult to check their validity or accuracy.

With these cautions in mind, it is better to keep the analysis as simple as possible. As a first step, simple totals and percentages may be calculated and this may be followed by an analysis broken down by different categories of respondent.

For example, the monitoring records of a micro-credit scheme may include records for each client of their gender, the loan size, and use of loan. The raw data may be presented as a table:

Client	Gender	Loan size	Business activity
1	f	1,000	Restaurant
2	f	1,500	Cattle breeding
3	m	1,500	Bakery
4	f	500	Vegetable trading
5	m	3000	Butchery
Etc. …			

Among its objectives, the project may be aiming to improve women's access to credit and promote the diversification of livelihoods. A first step in analysis is to calculate the average loan size, the percentage of male and female clients, the number of clients involved in each business activity.

This first analysis may show, for example, that 75% of the clients are women and this may be cited as evidence that the project is improving women's access to credit. A more detailed analysis might calculate the average size of loan given to women and men. This may show that although more women are taking loans, the average loan size is considerably smaller than that for men; the 25% of male clients may be using over 50% of the loan capital. This changes the picture dramatically and suggests the scheme may be struggling to achieve its objective.

Note that this relationship between gender and loan size will only emerge from the data if those carrying out the analysis look for it. Looking at results broken down by gender, age or other demographic categories is a standard way of reviewing data. Other ideas for what relationships to look for may arise from experience in the project, qualitative data or simple hunches. For example, you may suspect that men tend to get involved in businesses which require more capital investment than women. Breaking down activities by gender will show if there is a difference in the types of enterprises.

This may be very important in helping to interpret the findings. If men and women are involved in the same sort of activities, yet men still capture most of the loan capital, this may suggest that loan officers are using different standards for men and women. This may lead to a recommendation that loan officers receive different training or there should be a change in personnel. If the average loan size for men and women in the same activities is the same, but men are engaged in more capital hungry ventures, the problem may lie with the structure of the credit scheme rather than the staff. This may lead to recommendations to change the maximum loan size, restrict the activities eligible for loans, or look at training to bring women into these large businesses.

This form of analysis can be carried out on paper and possibly even in a participatory workshop – for example, tabulating the data in different ways on flipcharts – especially when the numbers involved are small. When large volumes of information are used, it is much easier to perform the analysis with a computer. For most purposes the analysis can be carried out on spreadsheets. Apart from calculating totals, averages and percentages, they can automatically tabulate data by different categories (for example, using Pivot Tables in Microsoft Excel). When more advanced statistical methods are being used, specialist statistical packages can be used (e.g. EPI-INFO or SPSS).

If a relationship between variables is shown very clearly through percentages and is verified by qualitative data, it should not be necessary to do further statistical tests to obtain further proof. In the example of the credit scheme given above, the relationship between the variables of gender and loan size comes across strongly without complex tests for correlation. Using computers, it may be very tempting to carry out sophisticated analysis using advanced methods, but this should only be done if necessary. Unless the person carrying out the analysis understands the methods properly, they may produce confusing results. Moreover, using these methods may make the analysis inaccessible to the wider group of stakeholders.

There are some basic errors that are commonly made in quantitative data analysis. Some of these are highlighted below:

- Think carefully before assuming that the people you have consulted are representative of the population. For example, if you interview people at a clinic, you may achieve a representative sample of those who attend the clinic, but you will *not* have a representative sample of the overall population.

- Differentiate between responses such as 'don't know' and no response at all. If 40% of people say that they do not know about the project, it is a very different result to 40% not answering the question. Be consistent about how you include blank responses in the calculation of percentages or averages.

- Make sure you are comparing like with like. For example, do not compare the average change in income over a six month period in one year with the change over a three month period in another.

- Do not calculate the average of averages to work out an average for the whole sample. For example, the average of {5, 7} is 6, the average of {7, 8, 9} is 8. The average of these two averages {6,8} is exactly 7. However, the average of the five individual data points {5, 7, 7, 8, 9} is 7.2.

Consolidating the Analysis – Interpretation and Attribution

The results of qualitative and quantitative analysis should be pulled together into an overall picture of the project's progress. As Figure 9 (p. 94) suggests, this may create a cycle as the different findings are compared and contrasted. Qualitative analysis may highlight particular relationships between variables, and this may require further quantitative analysis to verify if these relationships are reflected in the figures. Likewise, quantitative analysis may highlight significant differences between various categories of beneficiaries which may be explained by looking more closely at the qualitative data.

In order to ensure that the analysis addresses the questions posed by monitoring and evaluation, it may be helpful to prepare a table showing the indicators at the levels of output, outcomes and goal. Against each indicator, show how it has changed from the baseline or since the last evaluation and list the evidence for this change. Note that this might include some evidence which runs contrary to the majority – for example, not all respondents will say that their income has improved.

Include in the table an area for listing the evidence that does not relate to particular indicators but shows evidence of impact or other changes which were not anticipated. This table can feed directly into monitoring reports that are based on the project framework (see Chapter 1).

Indicator	Change	Evidence
Output – indicators of effort		
Outcome – indicators of effectiveness		
Goal – indicators of change		
Other results not included in indicators		

Such a table will summarise the changes relating to project indicators, but the analysis will not be complete until there is some further interrogation of the findings. It is important to ask why indicators have changed as they have, and in particular, how far these changes can be attributed to the activities of the project.

If the indicators have been well chosen and are specifically related to project activity (see Chapter 5, p. 66), it should be reasonable to claim the project has had some influence on the changes. However, such claims of attribution should be checked at this stage, in the light of the experience of the project and changes which may have occurred in the working environment. This task may be easier if a 'moving baseline' related to the situation of potential project participants has been established (see Chapter 1, p. 23.).

As far as possible a range of stakeholders should be involved in the interpretation of these findings. Findings may need to be reviewed and revised a number of times before consensus is reached between all the stakeholders. Questions which might be difficult to answer from the monitoring and evaluation data may be easily answered by some of the project beneficiaries. For example, the monitoring data might show that people in one village are not using the new well, which has been installed as part of the project, although similar wells are used elsewhere. This may be very hard to explain from the existing data, but discreet enquiries with some of the villagers may reveal that a curse has been placed on the well by an enemy. Such explanations for people's behaviour are rarely included in project management.

The interpretation of changes in indicators is of critical importance for monitoring and evaluation, as it will determine what lessons can be learnt. As noted in the example of the credit scheme above, different interpretations of the data will lead to different recommendations and actions.

Concluding the Analysis – Lessons and Recommendations

So far the process of analysis has taken the data collected to draw up a picture of the project in order to understand how it is progressing and to explain its progress (or lack of it). In order to complete the analysis, it is important to reflect on these findings and draw out any lessons for the future and recommendations for changes to the project or the NGO. Some questions which might be considered in the light of the findings include:

- Are there constraints to progress which can be addressed by the project – e.g. lack of staff training?

- Are there constraints to progress which cannot be addressed by the project – e.g. a change in land rights? If so what can the project do to minimise their effect?

- Are the project activities and outputs still appropriate – should some be stopped or others added?

- Are the project objectives still appropriate?

- Are there questions about the project's progress which cannot be answered by the current monitoring and evaluation process?

- Are there problems or solutions raised which might apply to other projects (run by the same organisation or others)?

Reflection on these types of questions should result in a set of recommendations for changes in the current project and the organisation, and a set of lessons which might be applied more broadly to other projects. For these to have a practical application, they should be agreed in discussion between stakeholders.

Where the whole process of monitoring and evaluation has successfully included a wide range of stakeholders, it may also be appropriate to include a set of recommendations for changes within other stakeholders – e.g. the community may take no new responsibilities or the local authorities may change their policy.

If the recommendations arising from monitoring and evaluation are to have any practical effect, they must be realistic. There is little point in recommending that the project's budget be doubled, if the organisation is struggling to raise funds for the basic budget. Likewise, lessons should be framed in a way that helps others plan their action rather than vague sentiments. For example, a conflict may arise, which forces beneficiaries to move from their homes. Drawing the lesson that forced migration undermines the project is not very helpful. However, lessons concerning how the project has adapted to the new situation may be useful in other settings – providing mobile services, embedding conflict resolution in other activities, etc.

Presenting the Analysis

Each form of analysis will provide knowledge which should be summarised in the overall monitoring or evaluation presentation. This presentation may itself take a number of forms:

- *Workshops* – often used for displaying the picture given by all the information to a wide group of stakeholders, especially project participants.

- *Meetings* – donors may request a meeting where the findings are presented.

- *Reports* – a report will be required as a written record of the analysis. The report is likely to be the last form of presentation as it will take into account the feedback from meetings and workshops. By the time the report is produced all of its contents are likely to be known by the main stakeholders and it may not be widely read when it is finalised. However, for future evaluations and to enable the findings to be more widely disseminated, the report will be important to pass lessons on to other projects.

Wherever possible the analysis should be translated into some kind of visual diagrammatic form for presentation purposes. The style used will depend on the audience and the nature of the data. Quantitative data is often easily shown as graphs and charts, but these may not be accessible to audiences who are not used to such figures. Some of the charts and diagrams used in PRA methods may provide some useful ideas of how to present findings using pictures and symbols rather than relying on formal graphs and tables.

CHAPTER 8
Data Use

All this effort of selecting, collecting and analysing data will be of no use if the work is forgotten and the reports sit unread at the bottom of a filing cabinet. This chapter is concerned with ensuring that data is used. At this stage it is worth recalling the reasons for monitoring and evaluation which were outlined in Chapter 1: accountability, improving performance, learning and communication. How do we ensure that the monitoring and evaluation system actually delivers these results?

Accountability

There is rarely a problem in ensuring that monitoring and evaluation data is used for accountability 'upwards' to managers and donors, since they will usually insist on receiving regular reports as a condition of their support. Ensuring that accountability runs the other way towards project beneficiaries and other primary stakeholders requires more effort.

A participatory monitoring and evaluation system will involve primary stakeholders at each stage. Therefore, accountability will be provided through the whole process. Beneficiaries and other stakeholders will see how the project is progressing and have a chance to provide their own analysis of the situation. They should be involved in drawing up recommendations to address concerns which arise from monitoring and evaluation. This makes it possible for them to hold the project management to account for implementing the recommended changes.

Improving Performance

If monitoring and evaluation is to improve performance, it is vital to have a system in place for responding to the recommendations that are put forward in both periodic evaluations and regular monitoring reports. As noted in Chapter 3, an evaluation should have a mechanism in place for following up on recommendations and taking appropriate action. The recommendations that arise from monitoring are likely to be more moderate and may be incorporated within the continuous project management – for example, where they are simply concerned with adjusting the activities for the next quarter, changing priorities or the timing of activities.

However, a good monitoring system is also likely to pick up any major concerns about the project, which must be addressed quickly. These may concern the NGO's management, for example, misuse of funds by project staff; or operational difficulties, for example, a credit scheme where loans are not being repaid. These may require an extraordinary response for immediate action or to investigate the issues more thoroughly.

It is important to strike a balance between implementing changes in the light of monitoring and evaluation and maintaining the stability of the project. Frequent changes in policy and management can create enormous difficulties for an NGO and a project. They are likely to undermine morale of staff and other stakeholders and may create more confusion than they solve. Sometimes, it may be better to allow things to continue to see how they develop. Some potential problems may become insignificant in time and there may be important learning points to be gained.

For more details about managing change see Fowler (1997). The following points (largely drawn from Fowler) should be borne in mind when putting recommendations from monitoring and evaluation into practice:

- Who will be responsible for managing changes? At what level of authority in the NGO will the changes need to be approved? Will the donors' approval be required?

- How will progress in implementing changes be monitored – through the usual project monitoring system (in the case of minor changes) or possibly through further reviews for more significant changes?

- How will the proposed changes effect resource allocation? Will staff need to be moved? Will extra funds be required? – if so, it may be more realistic to adopt them in the next funding cycle.

- What will be a realistic timescale for implementing changes? Can they be implemented immediately? Can they be implemented in one step or will they require a longer process?

- What resistance will there be to change – external opposition, individual stakeholders' resistance, organisational inertia? How will this resistance be dealt with?

Finally, it is important to remember that you are implementing changes in order to improve performance. It cannot be assumed that making the required changes will automatically lead to an improvement in the programme – in the same way that you cannot assume that producing project outputs inevitably results in objectives being achieved. Sometimes changes to the project may create other difficulties or simply fail to work as expected. It is therefore important that the change in performance is noted in future monitoring and evaluation – it feeds into the project cycle (see Figure 3, p.15).

Learning

Responding to recommendations to improve immediate performance may present less of a challenge than ensuring that lessons are learnt for the future. NGOs often find it very difficult to retain lessons and recall them at the appropriate time. If monitoring and evaluation data is to have a longer term use, the NGO involved must become a 'learning organisation':

> An organisation which actively incorporates the experience and knowledge of its members and partners through the development of practices, policies, procedures and systems in ways which continuously improve its ability to set and achieve goals, satisfy stakeholders, develop its practice, value and develop its people and achieve its mission with its constituency.[1]

This is discussed more fully in Britton (1998) but some of the key points from his paper are presented here.

Build up an Organisational Memory

It is vitally important the lessons which arise from monitoring and evaluation are remembered within the organisation. 'If learning is locked inside the heads of individuals, the organisation becomes very vulnerable if those individuals leave or forget! The old African proverb that "when an old person dies, a library is lost" should no longer apply within organisations in these days of information technology. A learning organisation needs mechanisms which enable an individual's memory to be "down-loaded" into an information system so that everyone can continue to access that person's experience and their analysis of that experience long after the individual has moved on to other organisations'[2].

Reports produced by the monitoring and evaluation system make a crucial contribution to the organisational memory. In a participatory process, by the time the report is written its findings and conclusion may be well-known to all participants. As a result it may be tempting to see the report as an extra piece of work, which will add little value to the whole process. However, as memories of the evaluation fade or new experiences push out the past, these reports are essential to remind people of past lessons. Monitoring and evaluation records may feed into future project plans and training materials or help in dealing with particular situations which mirror the past.

Ensuring the information is retained within the organisation is only one side of the story. Once it is there, it has to be readily accessible to others, if it is to be useful for applying lessons. In a large organisation, with many projects, the volume of reports and other monitoring and evaluation data may be huge. Monthly, quarterly and annual reports from projects based in different locations soon add up to hundreds of papers. Finding useful material will become impossible unless they are put together in some orderly way.

This may take the form of a library or paper archive where reports are catalogued by

---

[1] Aitken and Britton cited in Britton 1998.
[2] Britton 1998: 19.

date and project. Where a large number of projects in different fields are involved, it should be possible to cross-reference by subject. However, it would be preferable to have such an archive in a computer database as this will make it much more accessible. Rather than people coming to the library, the material can be disseminated to different project offices to be used throughout the organisation. A computer database would also have greater flexibility for cross-referencing and searching. Ideally, it should be possible to arrange a hierarchical database where top-level reports are linked to the source reports (see the Reporting Pyramid in Chapter 2) and even to the underlying data. Then a project manager dealing with a problem of corruption in an agricultural development programme, for example, may be able to search for examples of how others have dealt with it in the past.

Indications that an organisation is developing a memory include:[3]
- 'The organisation has mechanisms for "remembering" the experience of its current and previous work through the development of highly accessible databases, resource / information centres and data retrieval systems.
- All written reports and key documents are cross-referenced and made easily accessible to all staff.
- The organisation is not vulnerable to losing its experience when individuals leave. For example, staff who leave the organisation go through a systematically recorded debriefing to ensure that the organisation retains their knowledge.
- The organisation has a systematic database of all its project and programme work which can enable staff and "outsiders" to identify where expertise resides.
- The information function is given sufficient prominence and is resourced adequately to enable the organisation to keep its records up to date.'

Applying the Learning

The ultimate test of learning is the ability to apply what has been learned. Only when learning is applied in the work setting can we say that a continuous learning cycle has been created. For many NGOs, the application of learning is not limited only to their own organisation but also to the practice and policy of others through the processes of capacity-building, scaling-up and advocacy.

At present, many NGOs' scaling-up and advocacy strategies are based on what is probably a relatively small portion of the total knowledge and wisdom that they have at their disposal. In short, NGOs are regularly under-functioning.

Indications:[4]
- 'The organisation systematically uses its learning to improve its own practice and influence the policy and practice of other organisations or agencies.
- The organisation writes up and publishes its experience for a wider readership without using unnecessary technical jargon.

---

[3] Britton 1998: 20
[4] Britton 1998: 21

- The organisation has a strategy for scaling-up its impact which reflects the learning it has developed on "what works".
- The organisation changes its practice and priorities to reflect new knowledge and insights in its efforts to constantly improve its effectiveness.
- The organisation is constantly building its capacity and innovating based on what it has learned' .

Communication

Adopting a participatory process of monitoring and evaluation will improve communication between different stakeholders involved in a project. Meeting together, discussing project progress, and agreeing conclusions and recommendations will ensure that all parties are aware of the project's progress. However, in addition to the major stakeholders, it may be helpful to communicate results to others, who are not so directly concerned, for example:

- *Potential donors* – a clear and honest presentation of the project's progress will be of great value in funding applications to new donors. An intelligent donor will be more impressed by an application which discusses problems faced by the project and the response to them, than a proposal that only shows the positive aspects and hides any difficulties.

- *Individual supporters* – many NGOs have a network of people who offer financial and other support but may live in a completely different society, e.g. city dwellers supporting rural projects or citizens of Northern countries supporting NGO projects in the South. They may have no exposure to the lives of the project's beneficiaries and messages from the monitoring and evaluation exercise may help to make the day to day challenges of the project a reality to them. This may even apply to staff within the NGO who are working in support or management roles far from the 'action' of project implementation in the field.

- *Other development organisations* – the experience gained from the project may be helpful to other organisations working in similar areas. This may not only help them improve their practice but it may also enhance the reputation of the project. Apart from any benefits for the NGO managing the project, this may also be a great encouragement to the project participants, especially if it encourages visitors to come and see what is happening for themselves.

The means of communication will vary depending on the intended audience. Project newsletters which summarise monitoring and evaluation results in very accessible language may help maintain the interest of a broad group of people. Communicating with other organisations may simply involve disseminating the lesson learnt as discussed above.

Avoiding Useless Data

It is worth reviewing the monitoring and evaluation system to see how the information produced is being used. If large quantities of data are being gathered but are not making any impact on the findings, recommendations or action, it suggests that this data is not be used. Why is this the case? If it could be used, but for some reason is not being properly included in the analysis, try to modify the analysis to take account of it. Remember some data may only be useful after some time – especially that which reveals trends. Some data becomes more interesting when you go back to it – you may think nothing has changed but then when you look back at reports from previous years, you find that things were different then. However, some data may have no use within the monitoring and evaluation system and you should stop collecting it.

PART 3

Monitoring and Evaluation for Advocacy, Capacity Building and Humanitarian Emergencies

The general principles and guidelines described in Parts 1 and 2 of this book are applicable to many, if not most, areas of social development. In this final part, we consider three areas of intervention which present particular challenges for monitoring and evaluation: advocacy, capacity building and humanitarian emergencies.

These chapters describe the particular issues which mark out these three areas from other social development projects. The aims of both advocacy and capacity building interventions are likely to be contested – the former by external opponents and the latter by internal resistance – and this creates new challenges for monitoring and evaluation which are discussed in Chapters 9 and 10. Chapter 9 also highlights the particular difficulties in clarifying the objectives of advocacy, establishing the units of assessment and the major challenge of attributing impact to particular advocacy interventions. Chapter 10 looks at use of organisational assessments for establishing a baseline for assessing progress in capacity building. Chapter 11 summarises the challenges that arise from the fast moving and often insecure context in which the project is operating during a humanitarian crisis.

These chapters aim only to make the reader aware of the major areas of difficulty and to direct them towards additional materials which go into these issues in much greater depth.

CHAPTER 9

Monitoring and Evaluation of Advocacy

It is being increasingly recognised that social development projects can only have limited success as long as they are conducted within a local and global environment of gross inequality in power and wealth. Many organisations involved in social development are addressing this problem by engaging in advocacy programmes which aim to change this wider context. These may range from campaigning for the rights of farmers being removed from land by corrupt officials, to advocating for changes in inheritance laws which prevent widows inheriting their husbands' property.

Advocacy for social development can be defined as 'the strategic use of information to democratise unequal power relations and to improve the conditions of those living in poverty or who are otherwise discriminated against.'[1] It includes both campaigning, which involves large numbers of people in a publicly visible process, and lobbying, which is a more private process that targets particular individuals who are in positions of power to change policy. An important aspect of advocacy work is that it is focused on achieving a specific change in policy and practice. This distinguishes it from awareness raising, which aims to increase knowledge and change attitudes rather than bringing about changes in behaviour.[2]

Although the general principles of monitoring and evaluation described in Chapter 1should apply to advocacy interventions, they do raise new challenges, some of which are discussed here. Further information can be found in Roche (1999) and Davies (2001).

Participation and Advocacy

Throughout this book, it has been argued that those involved in social development must be accountable in two directions: both to those they aim to assist – downwards accountability – and to their donors – upwards accountability (see Figure 2 in Chapter 1). This is recognised as a critical issue in the case of advocacy work where organisations claim to speak on behalf of a particular client group. These 'beneficiaries' may not even know that anyone is advocating on their behalf, and they may have little influence on who speaks for

---

[1] Roche 1999: 1992. There is also a wide range of advocacy work that is not concerned with achieving social justice and in some cases may be advocating against it. For example, businesses and other interest groups may campaign against measures which would reduce their profits or power.
[2] Davies 2001: 14.

them or what they say.

There is a danger that external (often Northern) advocates can adopt issues or groups of people (especially in the case of minorities) as subjects for advocacy without consultation with these clients. This will undermine the whole advocacy process in two ways. First, the advocacy messages are very unlikely to be focused on the clear priorities of the client group and as a result the client group may reject them. Second, it is fundamentally disempowering for the client group and is likely to result in one form of inequality or oppression being replaced by another.

In cases where the policy makers, who are the target of advocacy interventions, sit in a different continent from the communities affected by their policies, it may be impossible to achieve the levels of participation described earlier (in Box 2, Chapter 1). For example, advocacy on issues such as international trade rules may be so far removed from the day to day lives of those who are trapped in poverty by the trade system, that it is only possible for a tiny proportion to have any involvement in the advocacy process. How can these beneficiaries be meaningfully involved in setting indicators for such an advocacy project?

Making the Objectives of Advocacy Clear

Establishing clear objectives for advocacy interventions is more complicated than for social development projects and they do not fit comfortably into the project framework presented in Chapter 1 (page 17). The activities may be quite subtle and difficult to describe as separate points as required by the project framework. The links between activities, outputs, objectives and goals are not straightforward, as the path towards change depends on the responses of those who are the target of the advocacy work. Unlike most social development projects, where it is assumed that those most intimately involved in the project will support it, advocacy work by its very nature must anticipate active opposition. The progress of advocacy is therefore critically dependent on the actions of those who have no stake in the project.

Although the overall goal of an advocacy project may remain the same through the project, the activities and outputs will need continual revision in the light of the responses of those targeted by advocacy. Any attempt to develop a project framework for advocacy must be even more flexible than those for other areas of social development. Despite these difficulties, some organisations still use the project framework for advocacy interventions, as it is consistent with the project approach they use in other areas of work. There have been steps to adapt the framework by adding two columns: one to list the allies and opponents at each level, and the other for policy targets at each level.[3]

Rather than seeing change occurring by the achievement of a set of objectives at the same levels, Oxfam uses a simple model of stepped objectives for its advocacy work as follows:[4]

---

[3] Davies 2001: 31.

[4] Roche 1999: 198. See Davies (2001) for further discussion of other frameworks for advocacy.

- Heightened awareness about an issue
- Contribution to debate
- Changed opinions
- Changed policy
- Policy change is implemented
- Positive change in people's lives

Whatever model for change is used, it is important that the objectives set at every level are clear and realistic. Many advocacy projects set objectives which are not measurable and are over-ambitious. Inevitably, the indicators to measure progress towards advocacy objectives will mainly be qualitative. They may often have to be proxy indicators, as the results of advocacy are often intangible (especially the intermediate results before policy change is achieved). This makes the monitoring and evaluation of advocacy more difficult, but the principles remain the same.

Establishing the Units of Assessment

Advocacy is aimed at a number of levels and involves a wide range of stakeholders. These include the end beneficiaries on whose behalf advocacy is being undertaken, the wider community, local organisations, staff from organisations involved in advocacy projects, the targets of advocacy such as legislators and civil servants, and journalists and academics, who may help spread the messages. This makes it more difficult to determine the appropriate units of assessment for monitoring and evaluation. Therefore, a clear stakeholder analysis is essential from the outset, both for planning the intervention and to design the monitoring and evaluation system.[5] In practice, it will be necessary to monitor advocacy in a wide range of ways. For example:[6]

Monitoring your target
- Record and observe changes in the rhetoric of your target audience. Keep a file of their statements over time.
- What are they saying about you and your campaign?
- Are they moving closer to your position, adapting to or adopting any of your language or philosophy?

Monitoring your relationships
- Record the frequency and context of conversations with external sources and target audiences.

---

[5] See Roche 1999: 205 for a detailed description of the pros and cons of using different units of assessment.

[6] BOND Guidance Notes Series 6 – Monitoring and Evaluating Advocacy
www.bond.org.uk/advocacy/guideval.html

- Are you discussing new ideas? Are you becoming a confidante or a source of information or advice?
- Are new groups or groups previously in opposition now talking with you?

Monitoring the media
- Count column inches on your issue and the balance of pro and anti comment.
- Count the number of mentions for your organisation.
- Analyse whether media is adopting your language.

Monitoring your reputation
- Record the sources and numbers of enquiries that you receive as a result of your work.
- Are you getting to the people you wanted to get to?
- How and where have they heard of your work?
- How accurate are their pre-conceptions about you and your work?

Monitoring public opinion
- Analyse the popular climate through telephone polling, or through commissioning surveys.

Problems of Attribution

One of the challenges of any monitoring and evaluation system is to establish the links between the immediate results of the project activities and the observed changes in the situation that the project aims to address (see Chapter 1, p. 19). Like any other social development project, changes may occur that improve the lives of the intended 'beneficiaries' but they are not related to the intervention. For example, a campaign on improving terms of trade for primary producers may observe a dramatic improvement in the lives of poor farmers when the world market price for their crops increases. However, such an impact may simply reflect market conditions rather than any change in the trading relations that are the subject of the advocacy efforts.

There are particular difficulties in working out the impact of advocacy interventions which are not found in other areas of social development.

- There is a two stage impact chain (as suggested by the Oxfam model of stepped objectives described above). There may be success at the level of policy makers which brings about a change in policy, but this does not necessarily mean that it results in the desired beneficial changes in the lives of the poor. This highlights the importance of being clear about the level at which we are looking for change – opinion, policy, practice or the lives of 'beneficiaries'.

- Identifying causes and effects is especially difficult in areas of policy decision making as the rationale behind changes in policy is rarely transparent. Policy makers may be reluctant to admit that they have been influenced in their decisions.

- The outcomes may be contested as different stakeholders claim different results. For example, politicians may want to give the impression that they are responding by giving high profile concessions in response to advocacy. They can then claim that the advocates no longer have any case to argue. However, such concessions may not address the underlying causes of concern.

- Advocacy takes places over a long time compared to other areas of social development so the effects take longer to show.

- Baseline data, or the lack of it, is often a problem. For example, on a politically sensitive issue it may be impossible to gain any accurate picture of the current views of the people whose opinions we are trying to change.

- Many advocacy issues are addressed by large numbers of organisations, especially when the issue is one of global concern, such as trade relations or weapons. Working in a network with other organisations is likely greatly to increase the visibility and power of advocacy work, but at the same time it makes it much more difficult to attribute the results to the work of a particular organisation – 'success has many fathers'.

Guidelines for Monitoring and Evaluation of Advocacy

To a large extent the monitoring and evaluation of advocacy requires the same guidelines as those presented for social development projects in Part 1 (see p. 11). The particular difficulties raised above require some points to be emphasised even more strongly.

- *Triangulation* – given the contested outcomes of advocacy, it is essential that data collected for monitoring and evaluation is triangulated (see p. 62).

- *Keeping things simple* – when there are so many potential levels of assessment for monitoring and evaluation, it is vital that the system does not get too complex.

- *Monitor and evaluate your contribution* – it is important not to neglect monitoring the concrete outputs delivered by your organisation because you are so caught up in trying to observe and record changes in the wider policy arena. If an organisation is to continue to invest its time and money in advocacy work, it will need to demonstrate that it can make a positive contribution – both to persuade donors and also to satisfy itself that its efforts are worthwhile.

The box below gives some critical questions which may be helpful in working out the links between the advocacy activities of a particular organisation and the observed impacts.

Audience	Client
• Who was supposed to hear the message? • Who has heard the message? • How did they interpret the message? • How was it different from other messages? • What did they do in response? • Have they heard of the sender? • How do they differentiate the sender from others who might be sending similar messages?	• If the clients are not already working with the NGO, how are they contacted in order to ensure that the NGO is acting appropriately on their behalf? • To what extent have NGOs who are involved in development projects explained their advocacy activities to poor people they are working with? • Has there been any attempt to get these people to rank advocacy work versus other activities that they might see as more relevant? • What effort has been made to provide feedback to the same people about the results of advocacy work? • What effort has been made to seek an assessment of their results?

Adapted from Roche 1999: 232

CHAPTER 10

Monitoring and Evaluation of Capacity Building

Unlike most social development projects which are focused on facilitating changes within a particular target population, capacity building is focused on bringing about change within an organisation. An organisation's capacity can be defined most simply as the 'capability of an organisation to achieve what it sets out to do: to realise its mission' (Fowler 1997: 43). Capacity building interventions are usually concerned with the many factors which contribute to capacity such as the organisation's people, finances, physical resources, internal procedures and so forth. Changes in these areas are expected to improve the quality of the organisation's social development projects.

An organisation involved in social development may be either the sponsor or the client of capacity building interventions. An NGO may be the recipient of capacity building input from a external donor, or it may initiate its own internal capacity project to improve the quality of its management and its performance. NGOs may also sponsor capacity building interventions with client organisations, such as community based organisations, which may have the potential to deliver local services in a way that is more sustainable over the long term. Capacity building can be a vital component of a development intervention to ensure that it achieves organisational, institutional and financial sustainability (see p. 42).

Although many of the principles and ideas described in the rest of this book can be applied to monitoring and evaluating capacity building programmes, there are particular points of difference which must be taken into consideration. Some of these are outlined below. For further details on capacity building and the difficulties of monitoring and evaluating it, see Fowler (1997), James (2001) and Roche (1999).

Keeping Monitoring and Evaluation Consistent with Capacity Building

One of the basic principles introduced in Chapter 1 (p. 11) for any monitoring and evaluation system is that it should build up the capacity of those involved. This is particularly important for a system for monitoring and evaluating capacity building. Capacity building aims to improve the performance of the organisation and its staff and this aim is shared with monitoring and evaluation.

The system must involve a wide range of stakeholders as active participants and encourage reflection and analysis within the organisation which is the target of capacity building. The boundaries between collecting data for monitoring and evaluation and the capacity building are likely to be much more blurred than is likely with social development projects. For example, a workshop may be organised for the organisation's staff to assess progress in capacity building. Such a workshop can make an important contribution to capacity building as it gives staff an opportunity to reflect on how they take the change process on further.[1]

Organisational Assessment as a Baseline

In order to measure the changes in an organisation's capacity brought about by capacity building initiatives, it is essential to have some idea of the starting point – how much capacity did the organisation have in the first place? A baseline can be established through an organisational assessment. This will assess areas such as the organisation's governance, mission, leadership, stakeholders, management and organisation, planning, personnel, programme development, administrative procedures, information flows, finance, and human resources and human resource management.[2] Examples of the type of questions which may be used and the data collection methods used are shown in Table 8.

Any such baseline must be updated as the organisation and the context changes over time. Many aspects of the organisational assessment will reflect the particular people involved and they may change over time (for example, the 'problem director' may decide to leave). As a result it is usually necessary to supplement any baseline established at the start of the capacity building project, with a 'retrospective baseline' which asks about the changes people have experienced in the organisation since the capacity building project started.[3]

Contested Aims and Objectives

The capacity building project should focus on only a few of the areas explored in the organisational assessment. It would not be realistic to expect any intervention to solve all the capacity constraints facing the organisation. However, the actual aims and objectives may be contested by different stakeholders.

Most social development projects aim to address particular issues which are recognised as problems by all the major stakeholders (e.g. low crop yields, illiteracy, unemployment). Since capacity building is focused on the internal workings of an organisation, it may often be concerned with problems which are less visible and may even be denied by some of the

---

[1] James 2001: 28.

[2] See Roche 1999: 235 for further details.

[3] See James 2001: 33.

Table 8: *Example questions and associated data collection methods for an organisational assessment**

Area	Questions	Instruments
Governance	• What is the relationship between the staff and the governing body? • Do members of the board come from diversified backgrounds? • Are board members related? • Are women more than 30% of the board members? • Does a written constitution exist? Are roles and responsibilities of board clear and adhered to? • Is the governing body engaged in making decisions about the direction of the organisation? • Do board meetings take place regularly?	Secondary data analysis – board reports etc SSIs with senior management and board members SSIs and/or focus group discussions with staff
Mission/ Goal	• Does the partner have a clearly articulated vision/ mission statement/organisational goals? • Do the strategy and plan fit the mission and goals?	Secondary data analysis – mission statement, strategy documents SSIs with senior staff
Leadership	• Is there a process for leadership development? • Are the governing body (and senior management) accountable to key stakeholders (partners, members, clients)?	Secondary data analysis of reports, staff handbook etc SSIs with board, senior management, stakeholders-representative selection
Stakeholders	• Does the NGO include stakeholders in the planning process – does this process address their needs? • Is there a process to review the community satisfaction with their activities and services? • Are men and women treated equally?	Review of reports SSIs with key informants Focus groups with different client groups (men and women)
Management and Organisation	• Does the organisation have an organigram showing clear lines of management responsibility? • What allowances are there for participation/ consultation? • What forms of mutual accountability exist with stakeholders (MOU, agreements, systems for meetings, liaison etc)? • Is there an appraisal system? • Do procedures and policies exist in written form?	Secondary data analysis policy documents, procedures manuals SSIs with stakeholders Focus group meetings with staff

* Adams and Pratt, INTRAC 2003

Area	Questions	Instruments
Planning	• Is there a strategic plan? When was it last updated? • Are there periodic (annual) reviews? • Are senior staff, other staff, stakeholders involved in developing implementation plans? • Are clients consulted or otherwise engaged in developing strategic and implementation plans? • Are plans reviewed in the light of information from monitoring data?	Secondary data analysis SSIs with senior staff SSIs with representative group of clients Possible use of observation of activities linked to SSIs with staff
Personnel	• Are procedures for recruitment and selection in place? • Is there a staff appraisal system? • Do the staff have the technical capacities required for the programme? • Are there established forms of communication between the staff, and between staff and management? • Can staff make decisions about the work they are responsible for? • Are there organisational gender or equal opportunities policies?	Secondary data analysis Review of staff work – diaries, reports etc Observation SSIs with clients SSIs and or focus groups with staff
Programme Development	• Are stakeholders involved in programme design, implementation, monitoring and evaluation? • Does baseline data exist, and is it updated regularly? • Are the staff skills and numbers sufficient for the work planned? • Are staff familiar with the goals of the programme and other important information relevant to their jobs? • Are the board and staff familiar with key programme and organisational documents?	Secondary data analysis SSIs with management and key stakeholders, board members Focus group meetings with staff (possibly also stakeholders)
Administrative Procedures	• Do updated and comprehensive administrative rules exist? • Do administrative rules apply to all staff? • Do all staff receive information about what the organisation is doing (staff meetings, newsletter etc)? • Do procurement rules exist (where appropriate)?	Secondary data analysis of documents, procedures – examples of how issues have been dealt with Mix of SSIs and focus group meetings with staff

Area	Questions	Instruments
Information	• Is there a management information system, does it collect relevant information, is it well managed? • Are there systems for receiving feedback from staff and stakeholders? • Are reports produced regularly, in the relevant languages? • Is there an annual report? • Are there quarterly, or monthly reports produced on time according to a regular timetable? • Does reporting meet the needs of different stakeholders? Are reports circulated and publicly available?	Secondary data analysis SSIs with staff (especially senior staff) SSIs with different stakeholders – representative group
Finance	• Is there a transparent financial policy? • Are there clear financial procedures which are adhered to (Finance manual)? • Are there annual / appropriate budgets for activities produced with staff involvement? • Are the accounts kept for individual activities monitored and reports produced? • Are regular financial reports prepared (trial balance, receipts and payments, expenditure / income, etc)? • Are budgets monitored? • Is there an internal audit system? • Is there a regular external audit?	Secondary data analysis review of auditors reports, accounts, normal reports SSIs with management/ senior staff and either SSIs or focus group meetings with staff (SSIs probably better)
Human Resources	• Do human resources development plans exist or are plans prepared according to needs assessments/appraisals/programme? • Does staff training relate to their job and/ or career development? • Are there appropriate gender/ethnic other balances in staff numbers and grades?	Secondary data analysis Assessment of organisational structure – current and over time SSIs with staff
Human Resource Management	• Does everyone have an up to date and accurate job description? • Are the staff regularly supervised (weekly, monthly, less….)? • Is there a performance management system? • Is there a staff development programme?	Secondary data analysis SSIs with staff
Other	• Are there regular staff meetings? • Is the work environment positive for women, ethnic and other minorities?	Review of reports SSIs and focus group meetings with staff

key stakeholders. The organisation's staff and those who may be beneficiaries of its projects may be reluctant to raise problems for fear of undermining their position. However participatory the process, at times everyone may collude in turning a blind eye to something which may be difficult to deal with, or be a possible source of conflict. For example, it is unusual for problems of leadership to be highlighted, as most staff will feel that there is little they can do to remove a prominent, possibly founding, director. The areas that are prioritised may be those where it is thought there is more likelihood that changes can happen, rather than necessarily being those posing the greatest problems facing the organisation. Therefore, it may not be easy to clearly state the aims and objectives of capacity building from the start of the intervention.

Open-ended Indicators

The lack of clear aims and objectives inevitably makes monitoring and evaluation more difficult. In order to take account of this, the monitoring and evaluation process will need to include open-ended indicators, which emerge as the project continues (see p. 76). The process of selecting indicators may also serve as an opportunity for clarifying the aims and objectives of the capacity building project. Because these are likely to be contentious, it is particularly important that there is triangulation to ensure the views of the range of stakeholders are considered. It will also be necessary to cross check the findings from group interviews with key informant interviews so participants have an opportunity to raise sensitive issues in confidence. The key questions involved in developing indicators are likely to be a selection of those used in the organisational assessment (see Table 7 above). The choice will be made on the basis of the priority areas for capacity building intervention.

Extended Impact Chain

In capacity building the links between the intervention and the eventual desired result are more stretched than those between outputs, outcomes and impacts for social development projects described in Chapter 1. James (2001) likens the capacity building intervention to a drop of rain which lands in water. This creates ripples which flow outwards to bring about changes at the internal organisational level of the target NGO or other organisation, and then moves on to affect the beneficiaries of the NGO's interventions. In this ripple model the size and direction of the ripple is influenced by (and in turn influences) the context in which it moves.

Monitoring and evaluation of capacity needs to show the effect of these ripples as they move away from the intervention. It is not good enough to show that the capacity building changes an organisation as desired, if that has no effect on what the organisation does. However well run and efficient the management of an NGO, its capacity will remain low if it still fails to make progress towards achieving its organisational mission. This makes monitoring and evaluation more challenging as it is hard to demonstrate that changes in the lives

Figure 10: *Ripple model of the impact of capacity building* (adapted from James 2001)

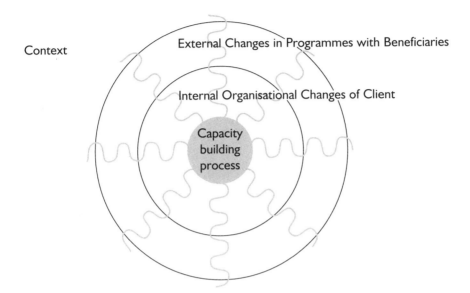

of the NGO's primary stakeholders are related to the capacity building intervention. In practice, it is only reasonable to establish a plausible association between capacity building initiatives and changes in the community. This may be possible by finding out from those in the organisation what difference they think the capacity building has made in the community where they work. This can then be cross checked by visiting the community and asking what changes they have observed in the organisation's work (James 2001).

Long Time Frame

Because of this ripple effect, the impact of capacity building interventions inevitably occurs over a longer period than be anticipated for social development projects. In particular, while the activities concerned with capacity building are continuing (i.e. during the capacity building project) you may only see changes occurring at the level of the organisation – the ripples may take a long time to reach the primary stakeholders. This must be considered when planning any evaluation of capacity building.

Low Key Processes

The objectives for capacity building projects are likely to be concerned about changing peoples' practice and behaviour and this is often achieved through training, mentoring and advising, which are notoriously hard to evaluate. Regular one-to-one meetings and discussions involved in mentoring and advising may be very low profile activities with limited immediate effect, but it is important that notes are kept of them for monitoring purposes.[4]

Training may occur in more visible events but it can be very difficult to evaluate. The short term review of training conducted at the end of a course or session is easy but not very informative. Evaluation forms from training participants may give some comments on the course, how it was led, the food, the venue, but as people sit and fill in the form before leaving the training venue, few participants can really assess the effectiveness of the training on their own practice and behaviour. Such reports are sometimes called 'dirty' evaluations in that often respondents will reply positively or negatively depending on extraneous factors, such as the quality of the last meal! To counteract the short term biases, the monitoring and evaluation system needs to look at the longer term effects of the capacity building.

---

[4] The contents of the notes should be agreed between the people taking part in the meeting, not simply produced by the mentor or advisor – this is important to ensure that confidentiality is respected.

CHAPTER 11

Monitoring and Evaluating Emergency Relief Projects

At times of crisis such as sudden natural disasters (floods, earthquakes, hurricanes), dramatic collapse of communities' livelihoods (drought, famine) or widespread violent conflict, an agency involved in social development may be involved in some form of emergency relief programme.

In the middle of a crisis, the focus of an aid agency's work is likely to be on delivering as much aid as quickly as possible to alleviate the suffering of those caught up in the disaster. Interventions may start very quickly and planning may be restricted to simply considering the outputs to be delivered – how many tonnes of food, to which population, by what date. At such times, monitoring and evaluation are often low on the list of priorities for all the people concerned. It is assumed that if aid is given then good is being done.

Unfortunately bitter experience in humanitarian emergencies over many years has shown that this simplistic assumption is not at all reliable. There are numerous cases where emergency aid programmes have largely failed to achieve what they set out to do and sometimes have actually caused harm. Reasons for this include:

- Providing the wrong or inappropriate aid – giving food which is unfamiliar to the people who do not know how to prepare it for eating, not using the right drugs to treat the particular strain of cholera involved.

- Emergency aid undermining livelihoods – the most common case has been giving food aid, which causes the price of food to drop, at the time when farmers are bringing their crops to market.

- Emergency responses undermining institutions – at times of crisis if the local community cannot cope with the situation and requires outside assistance, aid agencies can often adopt the role of being the experts, who take charge of the situation. This can sideline local institutions such as local government, local NGOs and CBOs or traditional leaders and reduce the capacity of the community to cope with future crises.

- Emergency aid diverted or used for political ends – aid may represent large volumes of resources in a very poor environment and it is a tempting target for those in power. In particular, in complex humanitarian emergencies where there is widespread conflict over a long period, there is the danger that aid can be used by one of the warring parties to fund the conflict.

- Emergency aid mismanaged – an organisation may start a small emergency intervention and find it rapidly grows beyond its capacity to cope. As a result large volumes of emergency aid (which may quickly exceed the usual level of resources available for social development) may be badly managed and used inefficiently.

Monitoring and evaluation is essential during an emergency programme in order to avoid (or at least minimise) such problems. It could be argued that it is even more important in these conditions than in a development project, as mistakes may have immediate and drastic consequences and any delay in spotting them may be very costly.

There is only space here to provide an outline of particular issues which must be considered in monitoring and evaluating emergency relief projects. This area is rapidly developing and new experience and resources are being continuously produced, many of them on the internet. Useful resources for further information include the Active Learning Network for Accountability and Performance in Humanitarian Action (ALNAP) www.alnap.org, which has produced training modules for the evaluation of humanitarian action that are available online; the Humanitarian Practice Network of the Overseas Development Institute www.odihpn.org; Wood et al. (2001); and Roche (1999: 164–91).

The main principles for monitoring and evaluation outlined in this book still apply, but they become even more difficult to put into practice for a number of reasons:

- Staff may be working at full stretch and find it difficult to put energy into anything which is not immediately concerned with delivering relief;

- There is often a rapid turnover of staff making it difficult to capture learning;

- The community may have very little capacity to participate fully in the project or its monitoring and evaluation;

- People may be displaced from their homes and moving around – this makes it difficult to assess any impact of the project on peoples' lives, as they may have moved on;

- The situation is likely to change rapidly making baseline information out of date very quickly;

- The project may be operating in an environment which is violent and with poor security;

- In a large scale emergency involving a big population, many different agencies may start operations – these are likely to be working with different goals and may undermine each others programmes;

- In complex humanitarian emergencies, stakeholders in the project may also be involved in the conflict – this raises many questions about how far different groups should participate in project management, monitoring and evaluation.

Some differences between the context of monitoring and evaluation in humanitarian crises compared to development projects are summarised in Table 9.

Table 9: *Differences between monitoring and evaluation in humanitarian crises and development projects* (source: ALNAP training Handout 3.3)

Characteristics	Humanitarian Crisis	Development Project
Context	Situation changes frequently/ regional level variations/complexity difficult to capture	Relative stability and predictability of the situation
Data collection systems	Difficult to construct timelines Absence of baseline information Gaps and problems in data sets Weakness of monitoring systems	Baseline data may be readily available Gaps in data sets may be addressed Weaknesses, if they exist, are not crisis related
Stakeholder context	Breakdown of institutions Polarisation and politicisation Trauma (potential problem for staff and victims) High staff turnover Lack of staff time Fatigue	Stable, not necessarily effective, institutions Less tendency for additional polarisation Populations able to cope
Security/ Accessibility Sensitivity	Access to areas is often restricted High profile media coverage – government sensitivity to media cover of some issues/criticism Extraordinary tensions	Access is not a hindrance Predictability of stance toward media coverage
Inter-dependency	Emphasis on co-ordination makes it difficult to identify specific responsibilities for implementation – hard to isolate an intervention from the broader context to attribute impact. Multi-disciplinary approaches result in diversity of staff composition and expertise	Lines of responsibility and authority for implementation are more clearly defined

Standards in Emergency Relief

With the growing recognition that the work of agencies in providing emergency aid must be monitored and evaluated, many NGOs and other humanitarian organisations (especially the International Federation of the Red Cross and Red Crescent and UN agencies) have put a lot of effort into developing tools for assessing the quality of their work. There is still considerable debate about what is meant by quality in the context of humanitarian aid. Some argue that it is only possible to establish good quality programmes by analysing the particular situation and deriving indicators on the basis of the specific context.

In contrast a large number of international agencies and academics have established the SPHERE project which has developed a set of Minimum Standards in Disaster Relief (www.sphere.org). These currently describe minimum standards in five sectors: water supply and sanitation, nutrition, food aid, shelter and site planning and health services. These are being continuously updated and are expanding to include new sectors such as livelihood security.

Whatever view your NGO takes of quality in emergency aid[1], it is worth noting that some donors may require that NGOs work to the SPHERE standards in providing emergency aid. These donors will expect monitoring and evaluation to consider to what extent these standards have been met.

Monitoring in an Emergency

In practice, the first stage of monitoring is likely to be situation reports, describing changes in the general situation, the project activities and immediate objectives. When the situation is changing very rapidly the reporting period may be very short – every few days – and this will gradually extend as the situation stabilises. The report may include the following sections:

- Changes in the situation since the last report

- Project activities and outputs since the last report – including problems faced and ways they have been addressed

- Changes to the project plan since the last report – including reasons for these changes

It is particularly important that as far as possible written records are kept of meetings held including the discussions and decisions made in the emergency. Because the external conditions may be changing rapidly, there may be frequent small adjustments to the project.

---

[1] The debate is summarised in Hilhorst 2002, and more information can be found on the ALNAP website www.alnap.org and the Overseas Development Institute, Humanitarian Practice Network website www.odihpn.org.

Through this process of incremental change, NGOs may find themselves drifting into areas of work for which they are not qualified or which run counter to their mission and values. Monitoring these changes in the project will make it possible to pick up such problems more quickly and to identify how the NGO got into this position.

Although the project may be started without a participatory assessment and with vague ideas of the overall aims and objectives, these issues should be addressed as quickly as possible. At the least surveys to assess beneficiary satisfaction with both the aid delivered and the process of delivery should be carried out soon after the project starts.

One of the weakest areas of monitoring at the height of an emergency is often the accounts. In stark contrast to development projects where every cent is counted, in emergency relief there may be sufficient money available so it is not a constraint on action – the chaos of the situation and lack of management capacity may present greater difficulties. In order to move rapidly, the normal controls on spending, such as authorisation limits on field expenses, may be relaxed. Unless they have accounts personnel in the field, NGOs often find that receipts and cash books are not properly kept. In a development project where spending may be relatively slow paced and regular it is easy to catch up on the accounts. In emergencies where large sums of money may be spent very quickly, it is very easy for large holes to appear in the accounts, so the NGO cannot accurately report on how it has spent the money.

Evaluation in an Emergency

In humanitarian crises, the distinction between monitoring and evaluation is even more blurred than with development projects, as the time frame is usually much shorter. If monitoring systems are not put in place immediately, an evaluation may be the first review of the emergency project. Some refer to 'real-time evaluation' as the ongoing review of emergency aid projects while they are continuing – this is in effect another term for monitoring (given the definition of monitoring we adopted in Chapter 1).

Because of the short duration of many emergency responses, it is very common to conduct evaluations as the project draws to a close or after it has ended. The purpose of evaluation will be much the same as those described in Chapter 3 (p. 40) with a particular emphasis on lesson learning for future crises. The evaluation may be the first chance that the organisation implementing the project has to reflect on its work and assess its impact. Where the humanitarian crisis has been very traumatic, the evaluation may also provide a useful opportunity for enabling staff to express their feelings and frustrations about their involvement.

In emergency relief projects, the usual criteria for evaluation described in Chapter 3 – efficiency, effectiveness, impact, relevance, sustainability – are often revised to reflect the context as follows:

- **Relevance/appropriateness** – replaces plain *relevance*. This is an expansion of the concern with the relevance of the project's objectives and goals to the priorities and policies of major stakeholders. Even if the project aims to tackle a relevant problem, does it go about it an appropriate way? In particular, in relief projects are the appropriate goods or services delivered – e.g. the right foods (essentials or luxuries)?

- **Connectedness** – replaces *sustainability*. How far has the project taken account of the longer term situation in communities affected by crisis? This is concerned with ensuring that emergency aid is not simply focused on addressing immediate needs without looking at the impact of their activities on the wider context. Food distributions may undermine markets creating problems for the future. Employing local staff for relief projects may pull skilled staff away from local institutions such as schools and hospitals, especially if higher salaries are paid by NGOs.

- **Coverage** – this is concerned with assessing how far the relief intervention reached all those in need and how far it met those needs. In particular, an evaluation should look at whether all groups were included in the relief project without regard for gender, ethnic, political or other distinctions. It will ask the question, did particular groups benefit disproportionately from the relief project? A gender analysis is vital for a proper assessment.

- **Coherence** – how did the relief project fit in with the overall aid response to the humanitarian crisis? Was there adequate co-ordination with government or other authorities, other NGOs, UN? This is important to ensure that the relief project was not duplicating the efforts of other organisations, contributing to the neglect of a particular area of assistance, or hindering other assistance through poor co-ordination.

Appendix

Case Study

In this appendix we present a more detailed case study than is possible within the main text. This illustrates how an organisation has developed a monitoring and evaluation system and some of the lessons which it learnt along the way. The information has been drawn from a range of sources but it is presented in a fictional form.

Background

FDG first came into existence as a project of a European based international NGO which intervened in response to the agricultural crisis in Relinesia. It was established as an independent NGO five years ago. Relinesia has undergone a period of rapid agricultural change over the last decade including land reform and transformations in the marketing of agricultural inputs and produce. FDG supports the development of farmers' co-operatives with the overall aim of establishing sustainable rural livelihoods. The organisation has a head office in the capital and four branch offices around Relinesia. Each branch office is involved in two projects.

Two years ago, FDG decided to introduce a participatory monitoring and evaluation system. Until that time the existing system had been very limited:

- Monitoring was focused on ensuring activities were completed and on time. This was achieved by field staff filling in standardised monthly reports for the branch managers. Much of the data consisted of numbers and lists – number of people, costs, dates and lists of staff and organisations. Limited narrative. These were consolidated into quarterly reports by head office and were then sent to donors.

- Evaluation only took place at the request of 'parent' INGO. Within FDG there was no budget and limited interest in evaluating the work. The few evaluations that took place were conducted by external evaluators after the end of the project. Much of their time was spent trying to work out what had happened during the project. It is thought the evaluations were generally favourable as the donors have kept funding the work but the full reports were never sent by the donor or INGO to FDG.

FDG felt pressure from both project participants and donors to encourage it to introduce a new monitoring and evaluation system:

- Upwards pressure – FDG ran into some problems in working with communities where the people complained that promised changes have not occurred. In some cases they started to refuse to co-operation with FDG and even threatened the staff in one instance.

- Downwards pressure – FDG was initially supported by its 'parent' INGA with very limited demands for monitoring and evaluation. The INGO tended to give regular grants but did not show much concern about the details of how it was used. Since FDG became independent, it has had to look for funding from other donors who have much stricter reporting conditions.

Introducing the Revised Monitoring and Evaluation System

As a result, the FDG management team, in discussion with the board, decided to revise the monitoring and evaluation system within the organisation. They recognised that developing such a system would take significant resources and applied to their founding INGO for a grant. Once the system was in place, the running costs would be incorporated within the budget of its overall operations.

When this grant was approved, it enabled FDG to appoint an M&E manager to lead the process of developing the monitoring and evaluation system. The person appointed was a specialist in monitoring and evaluation with a strong background in work with community organisations at the grass roots level.

> It was essential to have resources, both financial and human, dedicated to establishing the monitoring and evaluation system. This was only possible because the leadership of the organisation was committed to the process and without their support any moves towards participatory approaches would have been undermined.

It was recognised that introducing changes to the monitoring and evaluation of existing projects could be more difficult, so FDG did not try to introduce change across the board. Instead, it decided to pilot the system with two of the eight existing projects in different offices and extend it to new projects as they started.

Once the M&E manager had been appointed, her first step was to arrange a workshop with project staff to discuss the need for a revised system and work out how to establish it.

> It was important to meet with the staff first and give them a first say on how the system should be developed to make sure that they were 'on board'. The development of the system was critically dependent on their co-operation and if meetings had gone straight to a wider group of stakeholders, the staff might have been alienated from the process or even threatened by it.

Stakeholder Workshops

A one day stakeholder workshop was held for those involved in the pilot projects. This looked at:

- Stakeholders' views of the project's aims and objectives.
- The current status of the project – general sense of how the project was going and how far it was meeting its objectives. This was used as a lead-in to a discussion on the need for a revised monitoring and evaluation system.
- A set of key questions which can be used as a framework for monitoring the outputs, outcomes and impact of the project.
- A set of indicators to use at the different levels as the means of monitoring the project.
- The tools to use in order to continuously monitor and capture the results, outcomes and impact.

Taking this approach has an element of risk. Whilst it is essential to obtain the full ownership and involvement of project participants in the development of the monitoring and evaluation system, there was a possibility that they could say that the objectives developed (even with some of them involved in the process) and agreed by the donors were no longer appropriate or relevant.

Establishing the Monitoring System

After these workshops staff and participants in each project agreed to start collecting data on changes in the agreed indicators. Unfortunately the whole process was delayed as the donors had not been able to take part in the workshop and it was felt important to obtain their approval for the system to ensure that it would meet their reporting requirements. Despite the donors' enthusiasm for a participatory approach to monitoring and evaluation, it took a long exchange of correspondence for them to accept the new system. Fortunately they did give way, but this set back the start of the revised monitoring system.

Since the co-operatives already held regular meetings at which they took minutes, some of the information was readily available by passing copies of the minutes to the FDG office. Some other data collection was managed by staff making consistent reports of visits and meetings. In addition new activities of regular interviews and discussions with focus groups were started up.

As part of the revised monitoring and evaluation system, it was also agreed that there would be a review meeting of each project's progress at the end of each year. These reviews are based on the monitoring information and include project staff and participants, FDG staff from head office and where possible representatives of the donor. The reviews are informal and are supposed to provide a forum for wide-ranging discussion on all aspects of the project.

Outline of key questions, indicators and related tools for one of the pilot projects

Level	Key questions	Indicators	Tools
Goal Sustainable improvement in the livelihoods of rural households in the project area.	**Change** What evidence is there to show that there is improvement and sustainability in livelihoods? • How has the intervention affected the income of each individual member? • Has there been any increment in the yield? • How have the members/families utilized the benefits from the products? • How has the intervention affected the environment?	• Reported quality of life • Diversification of income • Household income • Crop yield • Market price • Household assets • School enrolment • Area forested • Water table	Community focus group Semi-structured interviews with co-operative members Secondary data (market prices, crop yields) Observation by project staff
Objective Members of farmers' co-operatives have access to improved agricultural services.	**Effect** To what extent are the interventions being used? • How many farmer members have linkages with extension workers? • Do members have demonstration farms? • Who are the people involved in the intervention i.e. description by gender, age, etc. • What does each of the people mentioned above do, and how are they involved? • What is the general perception of the members towards the project in general?	• Quality of interaction with extension workers • Number of demo farms and their use • Number of people involved by gender and age • Nature of involvement by gender and age • Co-operative members' views of project interventions	Extension worker visit reports Minutes of co-operative meeting Monthly reports Community focus group Semi-structured interviews with co-operative members
Output New agricultural interventions introduced to the area through the farmers' co-operative.	**Effort** What interventions have been put in place to improve livelihood? • What new products have been introduced? • What new services/activities have been implemented (since the beginning of the year)? • How have the members utilized the services? • What was the procedure of introducing the services?	• Number and type of new products and services introduced • Number of members using new services by gender and age • Number of members involved in voting for interventions by gender and age • Source of ideas for interventions	Staff monthly reports Minutes of co-operative meeting Attendance records at training Co-operative voting records Semi-structured interviews with co-operative members

The following lessons arose from the early experience of the system:

- There were too many indicators involved in the system. At a review meeting, which included project staff (including the M&E manager) and co-operative members, the number was cut back to two qualitative indicators and a maximum of three quantitative indicators at each level.

- Indicators which related to the lives of co-operative members showed change which could plausibly be attributed to the project. However, indicators of change in the wider community were strongly affected by external factors and were not very useful. The monitoring system could therefore only reliably show changes in the lives of the co-operative members.

- Although a wide group of stakeholders were involved in establishing indicators and tools, this level of participation was not followed through in data collection, which was nearly all carried out by project staff. Partly this was due to momentum being lost as the process was delayed, but there was also a failure to describe clear roles for project participants in data collection.

There needs to be some benefit in the short term for those involved in monitoring and evaluation. At the least the system must not be a drain on people's resources. Participation does not necessarily entail ownership and the more the system is seen as belonging to others, the less willing people are to put effort into monitoring.

- There was a great cultural inertia within the organisation for monitoring information to be sent upwards. Junior staff tended to be deferential and wanted to send what the boss wanted. Senior staff were not very interested in sending information back to the field as they never saw this as a priority. The M&E manager had to intervene to hold management to account for reporting to junior staff, and to encourage junior staff to follow through initiatives and challenge management.

This was only possible because the senior management of the organisation, its board and donors were publicly committed to the developing of a participatory monitoring system and had given the monitoring person sufficient authority and autonomy to follow up problems.

- At the start there were problems as the staff found it difficult to use the tools for data collection. As a result, the staff found the monitoring process a large burden and some of the data they collected was unreliable. In response, the M&E manager had to spend extra time with the staff until they had gained confidence in using the tools.

Introducing Evaluation

It was agreed at the stakeholder workshops that regular evaluation must be built into the new monitoring and evaluation system. It was agreed that each project should be evaluated at least every three years and FDG has started to include funding for this in all their grant applications. It was also agreed that evaluations could be triggered earlier if requested during a project's annual review and funds are available.

To date only one evaluation has been carried out under the new system. The first step in the evaluation was to hold a meeting with members of the farmers' co-operatives and project staff to establish the criteria for evaluation, particularly identifying areas of particular interest. These included issues such as the limited take up of new farming practices by women and addressing the concern that other interventions would have been more relevant for the community.

Using the findings of this meeting, the M&E manager prepared a draft terms of reference which was circulated to the project staff and project participants. Unfortunately, there was no formal system in place, such as a further meeting, to capture the latter's views and feedback was only obtained from the project staff in the time available. A final terms of reference was approved by FDG management and a team was recruited to conduct the evaluation.

The evaluation team included two external evaluators – a European male and Relinesian female – and two members of FDG staff – a man and a woman. The FDG staff were familiar with the project and the communities involved but not engaged in the day to day management of the project. One of the essential criteria for selection of the team was that each member should have experience of facilitating discussion and using participatory tools.

The strategy of using a team was useful in providing different views and enabling team members to learn from each other by seeing and hearing different perspectives. At the same time a number of learning points were noted:

- The involvement of FDG staff was beneficial as they brought a good understanding of the process and history of the project (as well as the people involved), a lot of which was not written down. However, on occasions they had a tendency to put words in the mouths of respondents as they felt that they knew what the informant would or should say. This became more evident as the evaluation went on.

- It was invaluable to have the Relinesian consultant, who was an older woman, on the team. Her ability to 'melt' into the background whilst visiting rural communities was a great advantage. She was able to sit and listen to what local people (especially women sitting on the periphery of a meeting) were saying and follow up with the occasional focused question. This worked especially well as this woman was a good listener.

- The management of an evaluation team is very time-consuming and needs time allocated to it. In this instance, the team would divide up into two each day and work in different areas. This created extra demands on the branch office as it had to provide transport in two areas. It enabled the team to cover more ground in the time available. The alternative of the team moving everywhere together would have made it more difficult to work unobtrusively in the community.

Afterword

This book is a distillation of the experience of a number of organisations in different regions, produced with the intention of bringing the learning points together in one place. It introduces the basic ideas of monitoring and evaluation to development practitioners. And it is a practical guide for field workers who are both committed to social development and also want to assess the progress of the programmes and projects in which they are involved. Hopefully it will help them to assess the impact of their work, enable them to gauge what their work is achieving, and understand how they could do things better. This book also offers an overview of some of the issues and innovations in the area of monitoring and evaluation. This is a rapidly changing field, and there are a number of different approaches to monitoring and evaluation being developed and new systems being introduced.

But it is also clear that it is not just the choice of system that is important, but also how it is applied. It is essential to make the process as important as the product – to create systems that reflect the dynamic and multi-dimensional character of what you are trying to measure. In particular, to create systems that ensure greater stakeholder participation in the development of objectives and performance indicators, their analysis and the dissemination of findings. Whilst such stakeholder participation is time consuming and expensive, their involvement is crucial if the ultimate purpose of such systems is to be achieved. It is therefore apparent that time and money is needed to make such stakeholder involvement possible. All the evidence suggests that successful evaluation and measurement strategies depend on significant investment of funds. The transaction costs of such frameworks are high, and if they are to be implemented successfully, donors need to cover the direct and indirect management costs and associated overheads. If this is not done, such processes will be poorly implemented, generate little information of operational value and suffer from limited credibility. One can conclude that only when monitoring and evaluation is seen as a valuable investment, not merely an operational cost, will such systems be seen as reliable, credible and trusted. It is then that development practitioners will see the real value of such systems and learn from their findings.

It is encouraging that many development organisations are now increasingly using different interpretative approaches to monitoring and evaluation. More of them are adopting participatory monitoring and evaluation systems, which emphasise the importance of qualitative data and we hope that this book will stimulate this trend. It is impossible to present examples relevant to every case in a book of this size, but INTRAC would be very interested to expand the range of experience that is available for sharing. If readers of this book will send further case studies or examples from their own organisations, INTRAC will endeavour to publish these electronically through the Internet. Please contact us with examples through the INTRAC website (www.intrac.org).

Bibliography

Books, Papers and Articles

Blankenberg, F. (1995) *Methods of Impact Assessment Research Programme. Resource Pack & Discussion.* Oxford: Oxfam/NOVIB.

Britton, B. (1998) *The Learning NGO.* Occasional Paper No. 17. Oxford: INTRAC.

Casley, D., and K. Kumar (1987) *Project Monitoring and Evaluation in Agriculture.* Washington DC: World Bank/John Hopkins University Press.

Cracknell, B. E. (2000) *Evaluating Development Aid: Issues, Problems and Solutions.* London: Sage.

Davies, R. (2001) *A Review of NGO Approaches to the Evaluation of Advocacy Work.* http://www.mande.co.uk/docs/EEDIMreport.doc.

Feuerstein, M.-T. (1986) *Partners in Evaluation: Evaluating Development and Community Programmes with Participants.* Basingstoke: Macmillan.

Frinton, P. (1995) *Statistics Explained: A Guide for Social Science Students.* London: Routledge.

Fowler, A. (1997) *Striking a Balance: A Guide to Enhancing the Effectiveness of Non-Governmental Organisations in International Development.* London: Earthscan Publications.

Gosling, L., and M. Edwards (1995) *Toolkits: A Practical Guide to Assessment, Monitoring, Review and Evaluation.* Development Manual 5. London: Save the Children.

Guba, E. G., and Y. S. Lincoln (1989) *Fourth Generation Evaluation.* Thousand Oaks: Sage.

Hilhorst, D. (2002) Being Good at Doing Good? Quality and Accountability of Humanitarian NGOs. *Disasters* 26(3):193-212.

James, R. (2001) *Practical Guidelines for the Monitoring and Evaluation of Capacity-Building: Experiences from Africa.* Occasional Paper No. 36. Oxford: INTRAC.

Marsden, D., P. Oakley, and B. Pratt (1994) *Measuring the Process: Guidelines for Evaluating Social Development.* Oxford: INTRAC.

Mebrahtu, E. (2003) *Participation, Monitoring and Evaluation: Perceptions and Experiences of INGOs in Ethiopia.* Forthcoming. Oxford: INTRAC.

Mikkelsen, B. (1995) *Methods for Development Work and Research: A Guide for Practitioners.* London: Sage.

Miles, B. M. and A.M. Huberman (1994) *Qualitative Data Analysis: An Expanded Sourcebook.* (2nd Edition). London: Sage.

Nichols, P. (1991) *Social Survey Methods: a Fieldguide for Development Workers.* Development Guidelines No. 6. Oxford: Oxfam.

Oakley, P., B. Pratt, and A. Clayton (1998) *Outcomes and Impact: Evaluating Change in Social Development.* Development Guidelines No. 7. Oxford: INTRAC.

Pratt, B., and P. Loizos (1992) *Choosing Research Methods: Data Collection for Development Workers.* Oxfam Development Guidelines No. 7. Oxford: Oxfam.

Roche, C. (1999) *Impact Assessment for Development Agencies: Learning to Value Change.* Oxford: Oxfam.

Rowntree, D. (1988) *Statistics Without Tears: An Introduction for Non-mathematicians.* London: Penguin.

Simister, N. (2000) *Laying the Foundations: The Role of Data Collection in the Monitoring Systems of Development NGOs.* Occasional paper 01/00. Bath: Centre for Development Studies, University of Bath.

Slocum, R., L. Wichhart, D. Rocheleau, and B. Thomas-Slayter (eds.) (1995) *Power, Process and Participation – Tools for Change.* London: Intermediate Technology Publications.

Wood, A., R. Apthorpe, and J. Borton (eds.) (2001) *Evaluating International Humanitarian Action.* London: Zed Books.

Useful Websites

ALNAP: Active Learning Network for Accountability and Performance in Humanitarian Action
Network of NGOs, donors, multilaterals and academics focusing on improving performance in humanitarian action.
www.alnap.org

BOND: Network of more than 275 UK based voluntary organisations working in international development and development education.
www.bond.org.uk/pubs/index.htm

ELDIS: Internet directory and gateway to a vast range of information sources on development and the environment, produced by the British Library for Development Studies.
www.ids.ac.uk/eldis/eldis.html

ID21: Research reporting service providing news of the best of UK-based development research around the world.
www.id21.org

IDRC: International Development Research Centre
A public corporation created by the Canadian government to help communities in the developing world find solutions to social, economic and environmental problems through research.
www.idrc.ca/index_e.html

IDS: Institute of Development Studies, Sussex
Leading centre for research and teaching on International Development.
www.ids.ac.uk

Monitoring and Evaluation News :Information about developments in monitoring and evaluation methods relevant to development projects and programmes.
www.mande.co.uk/news.htm

ODI HPN: Humanitarian Practice Network at the Overseas Development Institute
Network of academics and practitioners involved in humanitarian action.
www.odihpn.org